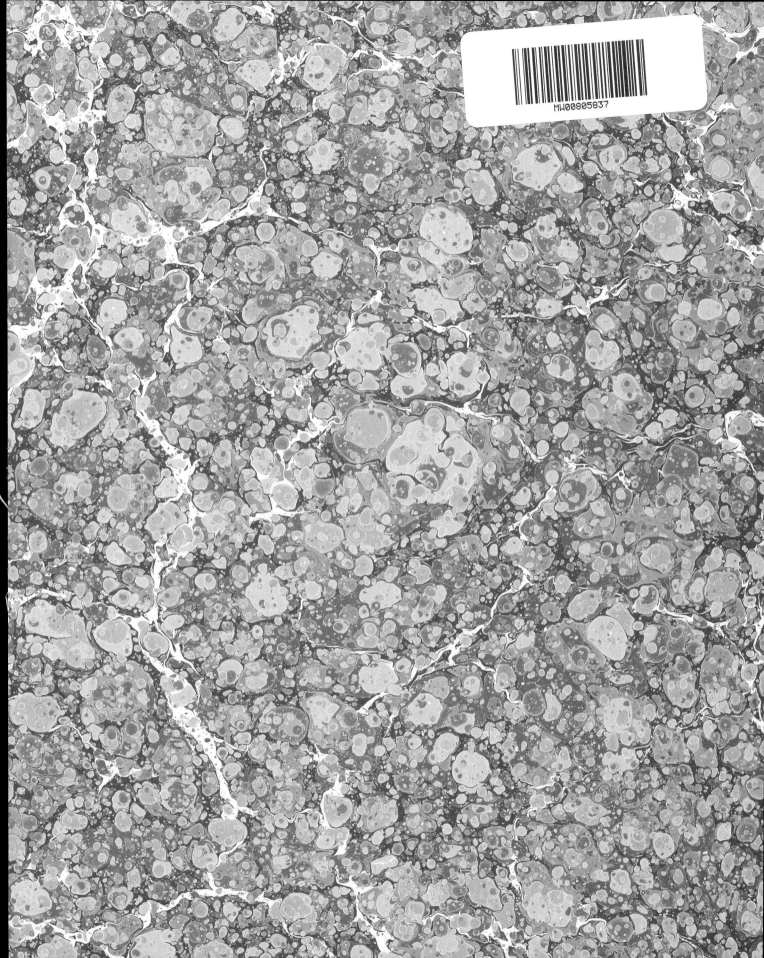

Marbled Designs

A Complete Guide To Fifty-Five Elegant Patterns

Patty Schleicher & Mimi Schleicher

Published in 1993 by Lark Books

Altamont Press
50 College Street
Asheville, North Carolina, 28801, U.S.A.

Design: Kathleen Holmes
Production: Elaine Thompson and Kathleen Holmes
Photo of cabbage leaf, page 11: Kim Rushing
Photo of stones, page 11: David Hastings

ISBN 0-937274-69-0

Library of Congress Cataloging-in-Publication Data
Schleicher, Patty, 1926-
    Marbled designs : a complete guide to 55 elegant patterns /
by Patty Schleicher and Mimi Schleicher.
      p. cm.
    Includes bibliographical references and index.
    ISBN 0-937274-69-0
    1. Marbling. 2. Marbled papers. 3. Marbling (Bookbinding)
I. Schleicher, Mimi, 1957-   II. Title
TT385.S34   1993
676'.234--dc20   93-10426
                                 CIP

Distributed in the United States by Sterling Publishing Co., Inc.
  387 Park Ave. S., New York, NY 10016
Distributed in Canada by Sterling Publishing,
  c/o Canadian Manda Group, P.O. Box 920, Station U,
  Toronto, Ontario M8Z 5P9
Distributed in the United Kingdom by Cassell PLC, Villiers House,
  41/47 Strand, London WC2N 5JE, England
Distributed in Australia by Capricorn Link, Ltd., P.O. Box 665,
  Lane Cove, NSW 2066

10 9 8 7 6 5 4 3 2 1

Printed in Hong Kong

PREFACE

As this book goes to press, I have been marbling for 15 years, 12 of them as a full-time professional marbler. Mimi came to help me "temporarily" six years ago, was promptly bitten by the marbling bug, and has been marbling full-time ever since. I tend to approach marbling intuitively and emotionally, while Mimi brings an innate sense of order and process with her into the studio. We are both enchanted with the color and pattern inherent in marbling and with the movement and magic that create the final result.

We want to thank Phoebe Jane Easton for her seminal work on the history of marbling, which has become indispensable. We thank Polly Fox and Dexter Ing, who, by publishing the marbling journal *Ink and Gall*, have taken on the task of keeping marblers in touch—a great gift after our years of working in isolation. We thank Carol Taylor, a true friend of marbling, for her skillful editing. And, last but not least, we thank all the marblers who have generously shared their artwork to be included in this book.

—Patty Schleicher

I was fortunate to learn marbling with the assistance of a nearly full-time teacher—my mother, Patty. I had the advantage of her 10 years' experience and so did not have to struggle finding solutions to problems she had already solved. I am not so sure I could have lasted through the challenges she faced in teaching herself with so little information available to help. I have had other teachers, and if they read this book they will undoubtedly find a familiar ring to some information given here. I am grateful to know other marblers who have shared a new approach or special trick—each has contributed to my growth as a marbler. My hopes are that this book will provide needed instruction for others to find their way with marbling—for we all marble with a different style, putting our personality into our creations. For those of you desiring to learn the mechanics of pattern making, perhaps this will be yet another stepping stone leading you to discover something exciting.

Much of my own marbling experience has been edition marbling of intricate patterns. Though at times this seemed monotonous, it taught me great discipline in pattern control, and I learned a great deal about color. Marbling, as you may know, requires patience and, of course, practice. If, perchance, you're combing a pattern from the glossary and you've made the wrong move or used a different comb than was indicated, don't be distressed. Perhaps you've stumbled upon something new. Just be sure to make a note of it so you will know how to repeat it the next time.

—Mimi Schleicher

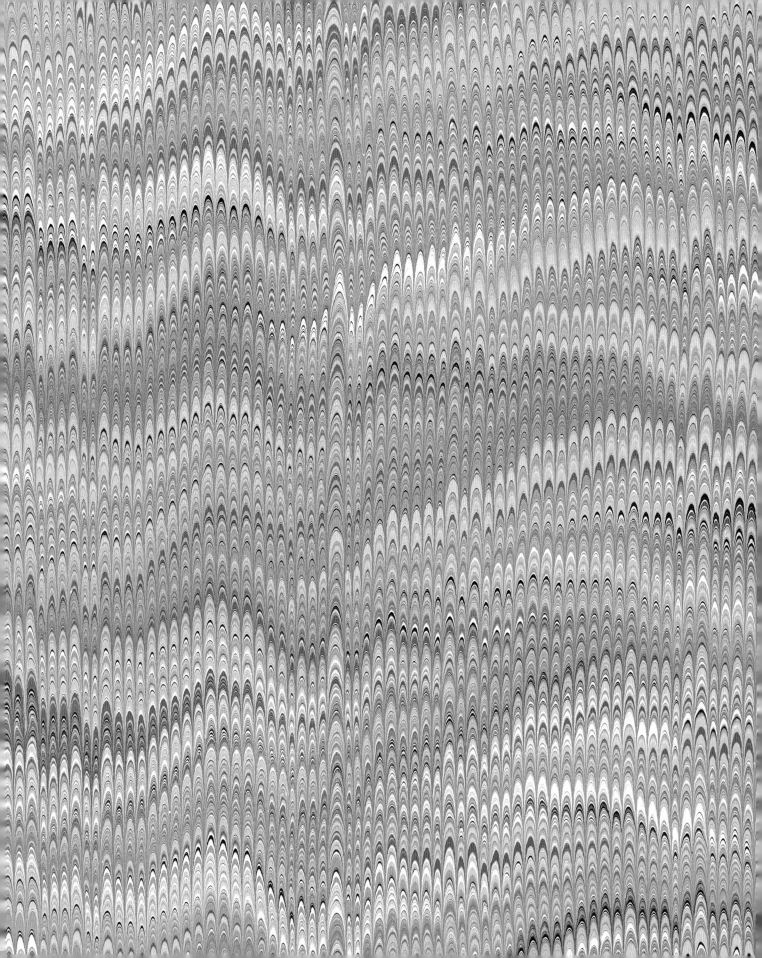

TABLE OF CONTENTS

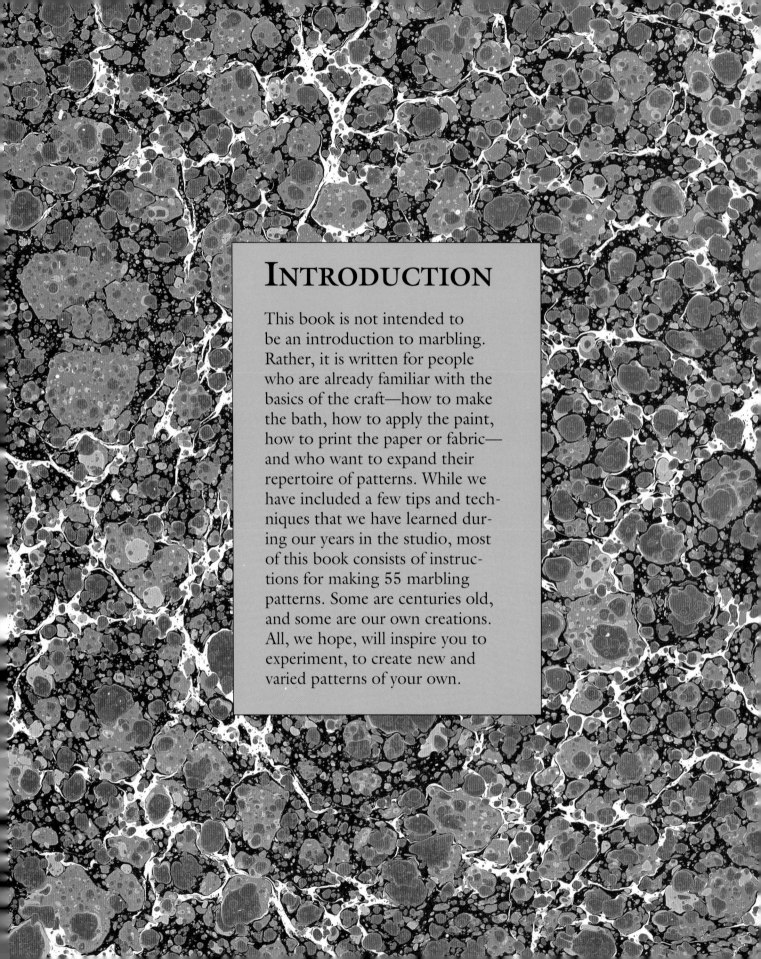

INTRODUCTION

This book is not intended to
be an introduction to marbling.
Rather, it is written for people
who are already familiar with the
basics of the craft—how to make
the bath, how to apply the paint,
how to print the paper or fabric—
and who want to expand their
repertoire of patterns. While we
have included a few tips and techniques that we have learned during our years in the studio, most
of this book consists of instructions for making 55 marbling
patterns. Some are centuries old,
and some are our own creations.
All, we hope, will inspire you to
experiment, to create new and
varied patterns of your own.

THE HISTORY OF MARBLING: A THUMBNAIL SKETCH

Even though marbling is centuries old, very few people know about it. Considering its popularity in various eras, its obscurity is astonishing.

TURKEY

In fact, the history of marbling is only now beginning to emerge. We know that a kind of watercolor marbling similar to that used in this book was done in Turkey in the 15th century. There are examples of *ebru*, as Turkish marbling is called, dating back to 1447 in the Topkapi Museum in Istanbul. Although Turkey is widely considered the birthplace of watercolor marbling, our knowledge of its origin is scanty. A lot of history was erased by Genghis Khan and his hordes. When the Great Mosque of Bokhara was destroyed in 1220, manuscripts from the library were torn up to provide litter for the horses. Again in the 14th century Tamerlane made a devastating passage through the area, destroying anything that Genghis Khan may have missed. We can only speculate about how many marbled papers and how much priceless information about the craft were destroyed. We do know that papermaking technology came into Western Europe via Turkey, and that the first paperworks were established in Italy in the 13th century.

INDIA

Christopher Weimann, an American marbler, also traced marbling to Persia (present-day Iran), where it was called *abri*, and farther east into southern India, where it was referred to as *abar*. Weimann studied and re-created a series of marblings done in the Deccan province of India around 1650, which he found in public and private collections in the United States, Turkey, and India. Weimann revolutionized the accepted theory of the pictures' creation. While they were once thought to be collages made of small bits of different marblings, Weimann demonstrated that they are indeed integral pieces of marbling created through the use of positive and negative stencils, resists, and a series of repeated marblings. The paintings demonstrate the use of pattern against pattern consistent with the design history of the East and the Middle East.

Christopher Weimann re-created several 17th-century Indian marbled pictures, including this pensive young woman.

JAPAN

In Japan there is a different marbling technique, known as *suminagashi*. Examples of this type of marbling date back to the 10th century. Suminagashi uses traditional Japanese materials, such as sumi inks and a surfactant made from pine tree resin. It is usually done on rice paper or silk. It has a history of use as a background for calligraphy—particularly poetry—and stylistically is expressive of the Japanese aesthetic.

These facts led scholars to speculate that marbling originated in China, but there is no hard evidence to support that supposition at this time.

ITALY

Over many centuries, as art, science, and technology worked their way west, they usually came into Europe through the great port city of Venice. We know there were marblers working in Venice early in the 16th century. Their papers were known as Domino Papers—an unusual name perhaps derived from the name of a cloak that concealed the wearer. (The game of dominoes came later, in the 18th century.) The name could be a reference to the secret nature of marbling, for it has certainly been a secret art from the beginning. Because of this Venetian history of marbling, many Italians believe that marbling began in their country.

FRANCE

In the 16th century the French developed a marbling industry and created a demand for marbled products, particularly books bound with marbled papers. French books have always been known for their beauty and craftsmanship. French book binders often used two different but complementary papers, one for the cover and the other for the end papers.

Marbled papers have been found on the walls of old buildings in Paris—small papers only a few inches square, which were bought and put there for the decorative effect. In the 16th and 17th centuries, Europe must have been a very gray world—smoky interiors with little light and linsey-woolsey clothing. The color that was available was for the rich and royal. The common people found delight in these small bits of color and used them to brighten their world.

The French tried to restrict this lucrative trade, first using trade guilds and then various rules aimed at controlling marblers. They exported quantities of marbled papers. Many French people also believe that marbling originated in their country.

HOLLAND

The Dutch were also active marblers, and it was from Holland that the British learned to appreciate marbling. Dutch toys were exported to England wrapped in marbled papers in an attempt to avoid the high duties levied on marbled goods. After these papers were carefully unwrapped and pressed, they were used to bind books. There are examples of books that have the boards lined with small pieces of several of these papers—all carefully pieced into place.

GERMANY

From the 17th century until World War I, Germany had a very prolific *buntpapier* industry that decorated papers in several different ways, including marbling, for domestic use and for export. Marbled paper was known as *Turkish*—a very accurate name that was often discounted, because Turkish was an often-used adjective that meant "exotic."

Wherever marbling surfaced, it became popular. In each country, there was a period in which it was stylish and in high demand. The fact that so many countries claim to have originated marbling is not surprising to a marbler. The sense of discovery inherent in the marbling process draws one in—and each marbler makes the process his own. Each marbler discovers the process anew and claims it.

A collection of antique marbled books.

MARBLING AND BOOKS

The history of marbling parallels the history of books. With the invention of the printing press in the 15th century, the art of printing spread over Europe rapidly. As books became more and more available to a larger and larger reading public, this demand created a need for quicker, cheaper binding techniques than the full leather binding over wooden boards that was customary with early printed books. Because of their brilliant colors, interesting patterns, and affordable costs, marbled papers were used to cover inexpensive books and as end papers for more expensive ones.

We have a good historical review of marbling from the books in which it was used, all conveniently dated, with the country of publication identified. Libraries and museums are now being encouraged to save the marbling from books being rebound to add to this historical record. There is beginning to be some interest in cataloging examples of marbling so they can be more readily accessed. Usually, even in a very tattered and worn volume, the marbling inside will be bright and well preserved. Indeed, binding marbled papers into books is one of the best ways to preserve them even today, because they will be well protected and will retain their beauty much longer than when used otherwise.

MARBLING AND FORGERY

Marbling has another quality that has historically made it desirable: it is tamper proof. Officials of the Ottoman Empire used marbled paper for their official documents until early in this century—which is one reason they kept the marbling process secret. If papers could not be marbled, official documents could not be forged. The marbled background paper also prevented the documents from being altered, since any erasure would be immediately apparent. In the United States, Benjamin Franklin, a printer by trade, convinced Congress to marble paper money at one end, in an effort to prevent forgery.

Until the computer superseded the ledger, it was usual for ledgers to have marbled edges. There were even traditional patterns for different kinds of bookkeeping—for example, nonpareil for single entry. If a page was removed from the ledger, the marbled edge pattern revealed the theft, thus keeping accountants honest.

Marbling and Religion

Aside from these practical considerations, marbling has a religious significance in the world of Islam. Hikmet Barutcugil, a Turkish marbler, makes it clear that to him marbling is an expression of his religious faith and is a religious experience in itself. At the Second International Marblers' Gathering in 1992, he related marbling to the wholeness of Allah and the unity of creation. He marbled flowers during a demonstration period, re-creating a traditional Turkish design. In discussing a tulip he had marbled, he mentioned that the way it was leaning denoted modesty—a subtlety foreign to Western sensibilities and an indication that there is a whole language of feeling in traditional Turkish marbling that is not part of a Western understanding.

In the Islamic world it is considered irreverent to portray life, particularly the human form, in a realistic manner. Only Allah can create life. In studying art and architecture from Islamic countries, one finds elaborate arabesques—stylized designs based on flowers, foliage, fruit, or even animal or figural motifs—in tile work that sometimes covers the whole of a mosque. Fretwork for window screens, which cut the glare of the sun but allow the passage of air, is usually geometrical in design. Persian rugs in all their glory portray abstract designs based on foliage and flower images, rich color, and a tradition of multiple borders. Marbling, with its elaborate patterns and rich colors, fits in well with this decorative tradition. It also provides a background for poetry and calligraphy, both important arts in Middle Eastern Arab lands.

The Universal Appeal of Marbling

Wherever it has been introduced, marbling has become popular. It is interesting to speculate about the elements of marbling that make it so universally loved.

Water

In virtually all the world's religions, the sacramental nature of water is recognized. This is expressed in baptism in Christianity, in ritual washing in Islam and Judaism.

In the Moslem tradition, there are seven levels of paradise. This belief is often expressed as multiple borders around the central panel in Persian prayer rugs. All levels of Moslem paradise contain two precious elements: flowers and water. (Desert people know the value of water as few others do.) As marbling has flowerlike forms and the water movement is visible in the completed pattern, marbling becomes a reminder of paradise to devout and knowing eyes.

The writer Theodor Schwenk states that water is the sensing organ of the earth, that this function is duplicated in our bodies, which are mostly water, and that the pattern of flow through our bodies is the same as the flow of water through the earth. Marbling helps us rekindle a reverence for water. It visually reminds us of this precious element and its importance to life itself.

Creation

Most religions have a theory of creation, of how order was brought out of chaos. The human psyche seems to seek order. Marbled patterns are an expression of that order—appearing on the marbling tray out of the chaos of the random sprinkles of color. Evidence of this randomness remains within the ordered pattern, creating the dynamic effect present in marbling.

Pattern

Nature is full of patterns—from the images of earth we know from space photographs to the weather patterns we see on television weather maps. There is a mathematical correlation between the swirl of a weather front, the curve of a seashell, the shape of our outer ear, and the double helix of our DNA. These are the same swirls a marbler activates in the water and captures in color on paper.

Small wonder then that something in a marbled pattern touches something universal within ourselves and creates a response—a gesture from within toward the universe without.

Do all these elements explain the appeal, the mystique of marbling? Do they help explain why a marbler feels that in the process of marbling he or she is participating in creation? It is most certainly true that in creating a marbled pattern, one goes with the flow—or it doesn't work.

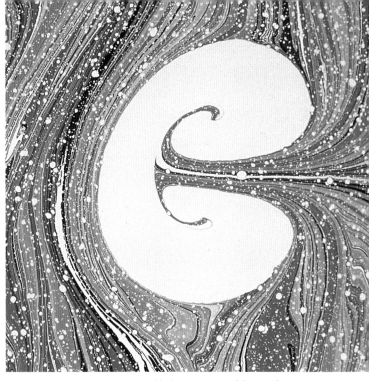

This random swirl of marbled paint created by a stylus resembles a weather front, a seashell, and the human ear.

The veins on a cabbage leaf are among the myriad patterns found in nature.

Perhaps nowhere does marbling duplicate nature so closely as in the stone patterns (see page 14).

11

GLOSSARY

The patterns in this glossary are organized into four sections: stones, getgels, nonpareils, and chevrons. For each pattern there are two marbled samples, always in different colors, usually in different scales.

PATTERN INSTRUCTIONS

Step-by-step instructions are provided in paragraph form for each pattern. In addition, diagrams for each pattern indicate the order of the steps, the direction of combing, and the pattern-making tool to be used. NOTE: If the size of the tool is specified on the diagram, it is the proper size for the large marbled sample shown on the left. If a different size tool is needed for the small marbled sample, that is specified in the text. The broken lines on the diagrams represent the previous step.

PATTERN NAMES

Some of the patterns in this glossary are historical ones, although we may not have reproduced them precisely the way earlier marblers would have. These are identified by their traditional names. When we did not know a historical name, we named the pattern ourselves, sometimes describing it by the sequence of combings that produce it—for example, "cabled chevron." When a marbler discovers a pattern, it seems to require an identity, which is how a pattern can end up with multiple names. There seems to be no central "marbling committee" to straighten out this jumble. Perhaps anyone who discovers and names a new pattern should send out a memo to let the rest of us know!

REPRODUCING THE PATTERNS

The designs featured in this glossary were marbled with watercolor marbling inks, or paints, on a carragheenan bath, using broomcorn whisks and homemade combs and rakes. (The one exception was a purchased brass comb.) Tools included three rakes: one with 1" (2.5 cm) spaces between the teeth, one with 2" (5 cm) spaces, and one with 3" (7.5 cm) spaces. Several combs were used: 1/8"

(3 mm), 1/4" (6 mm), 3/8", 1/2" (1 cm), 1" (2.5 cm), and 1-1/2" (4 cm).

We distinguish between rakes and combs, not on the spacing between the teeth, but on the *thickness* of the teeth. The hair-curler pins used for rakes create more of a drag as they move through the paints than do the slender metal pins used in combs.

TIPS ON TOOLS

Tools of various sizes can be used to make these patterns. What is extremely important is that the tools properly fit the marbling tray, which is one reason most marblers make their own tools. If combs are too short, their movement will create a wave around the ends of the comb, which will distort the pattern. If combs are too long, it will be impossible to move them at right angles to the side of the tray. If a comb is to be used in an undulating wave—for example, a bouquet comb—it must be short enough to move from side to side down the tray.

The length of the rakes is less critical, as the spaces between their teeth are wide enough for them to hang over the edge of the tray. Even so, it is useful to construct rakes with removable pins, so that one can be easily slipped out if it hits the side of the tray. Rakes should be the length of the bath plus one space plus room on the ends for your hands to grasp it.

Bouquet combs can be made any size. The pins must be equally spaced, making equilateral triangles across the comb. They should be shorter than the marbling tray by twice the spacing of the pins.

More patterns are possible if you have combs scaled for use on both the width and the length of the bath. For example, some patterns in this glossary are done over a vertically combed nonpareil; others are done over a nonpareil that is combed horizontally.

It is desirable to have more than one stylus, as different sizes create differing effects. Anodized aluminum knitting needles work well and come in many sizes. A wooden dowel can be sharpened in a pencil sharpener and will have more drag than the knitting needles.

It is very worthwhile to make marbling combs with accurate spacing between the teeth, and to make them well enough so they can withstand the rigors of use. Brass pins don't rust and are easier to clean, so they last longer than steel pins. Balsa wood, available in craft shops, is easily scored to mark the spaces for the pins. The pins can be secured between two pieces of balsa with hot glue, five-minute epoxy, a silicone compound used to repair tile work, or white glue, which takes longer

to set up. The combs can be strengthened by wrapping them lengthwise with strapping tape, which helps keep the dampness out of the wood and also makes them stronger and easier to clean.

READING A PATTERN

As you become more experienced in marbling, it becomes easier to read a pattern, and thus to re-create it—even without any instructions to go by. You must read it backwards. The last stroke will be boldest or most apparent. The next-to-last stroke will be the second most obvious, and so on through the pattern.

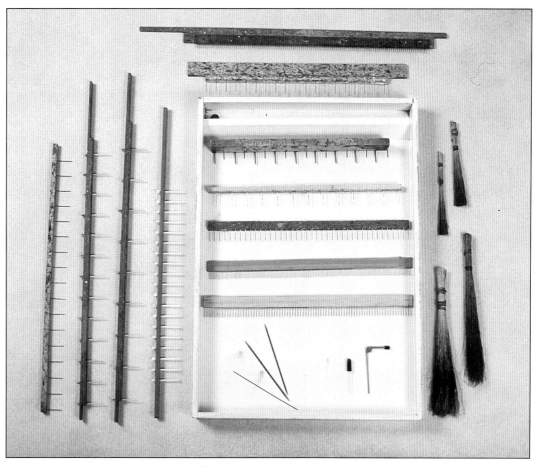

A marbling tray and a collection of tools:
whisks, combs, rakes, styluses, and an atomizer.

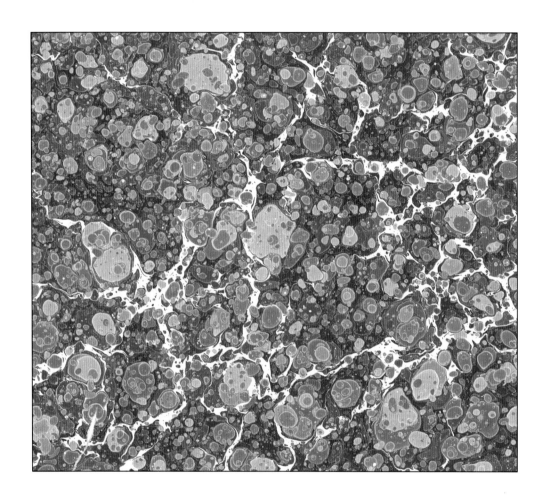

STONE

Stone, pebble, agate, rock, and Turkish are all names for this pattern. At first glance, the stone pattern appears simple—just sprinkle the colors on the bath and print it off. However, a great many variations are possible. A marbler's appreciation of the stone pattern grows with time, and many marblers consider it their favorite.

One variable is the age of the bath. Stone is not a pattern to do on a brand new bath, as the edges of the stones are often rough until the bath is more mature. Some marblers do stone patterns only on a spoiled bath or one that is starting to spoil. Choice of colors plays a major role. In stone patterns the first paint applied, called the ground color, becomes the veining color, while the last paint applied, known as the body color, becomes dominant in the finished piece.

Additives to the paint make a difference. Adding extra ox gall expedites rapid coverage. Sometimes one color is used with increasing amounts of gall. Other additives create specific effects—turpentine, spirits of soap, even olive oil.

The tools for applying the paint also change the stones. Large whisks with a lot of feathery broomcorn produce excellent effects, but they also require larger jars for the inks. Because of this, and because the inks have extra gall in them, we keep separate paints for stone patterns.

The paints can be applied to the whisks by eye dropper, so that one whisk has several colors. Another choice is to dip two or three whisks in different colors, hold them in one bunch, and wield them as a single tool. Some of the drops of paint will blend before they hit the bath, forming new colors.

Whatever the chosen applicator, it is important to cover the bath very quickly after skimming to minimize the chances of a skin forming on the bath. A skin not only will distort the stones but will keep the paints from covering the bath well, resulting in more of the paper showing between the stones.

The way the paper is laid can vary the look. Moiré Spanish, in which the paper is laid in a rock-and-drag kind of motion, is most often done over stones. In these patterns the last stones laid are large. The shading will be noticed on the large stones but not on the veining, giving the pattern a three-dimensional look.

Finally, a stylus or rake can be drawn through the stones, distorting them and making pattern lines, while the background remains stone-patterned. The best known of these patterns is snail, or curl. Surprisingly delicate effects can be achieved by drawing through stones.

It is small wonder that few marblers ever decide they've exhausted the possibilities of the stone pattern.

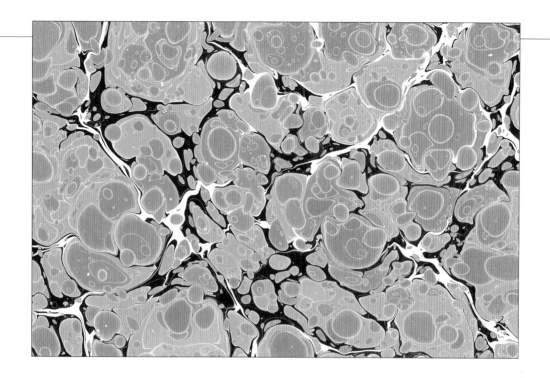

▪ S T O N E ▪

Using a regular or medium-size whisk, quickly cover the surface of the bath with the ground color (the first color thrown). Follow with the other colors of choice. The paints for stone patterns may need to be adjusted with more ox gall. As the surface of the bath is taken up with each color thrown, the paints added later need more ox gall to expand. Some marblers adjust the paints so that the second color has more gall than the first, the third more than the second, and so on.

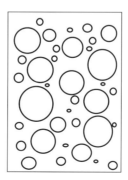

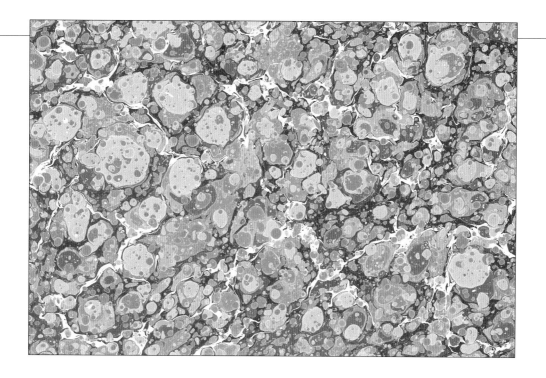

■ S T O N E ■

Colored paper can add richness to a marbled piece. The large sample at left was marbled on burgundy paper. The smaller sample, done on off-white paper, is a multicolored stone with seven colors. Keep in mind that the color of the paints will blend with the color of the paper. Both of these patterns were made using a giant whisk with feathery, untrimmed tips. Even when it seems that no more paint is falling from a whisk, look closely—there may still be tiny stones falling on the bath.

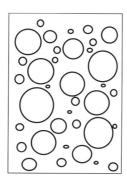

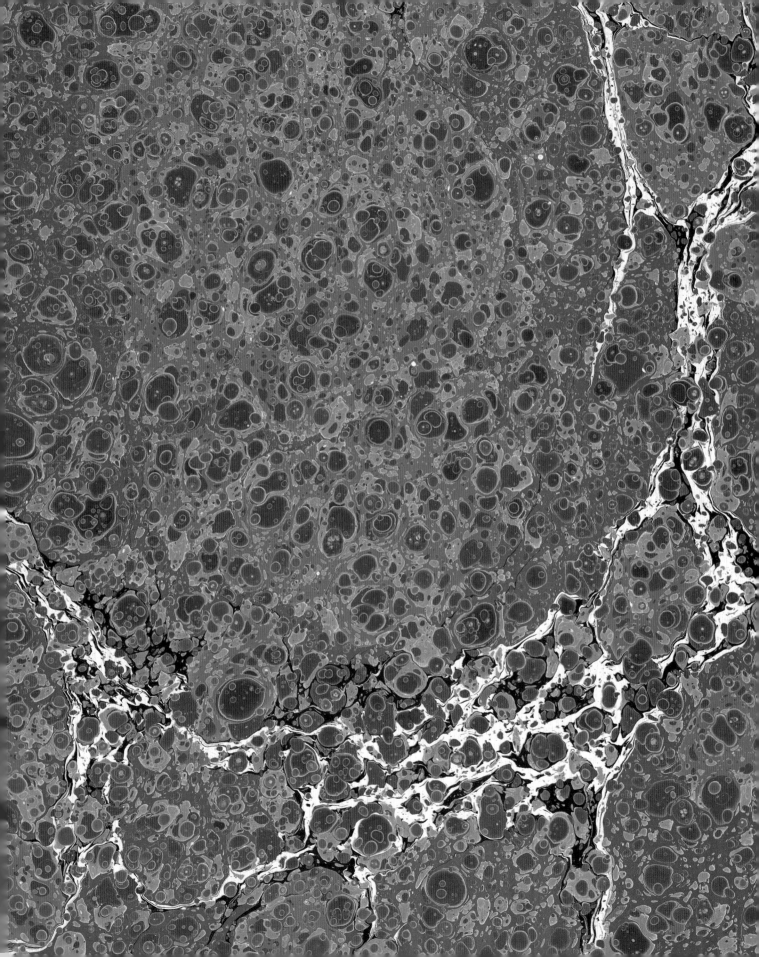

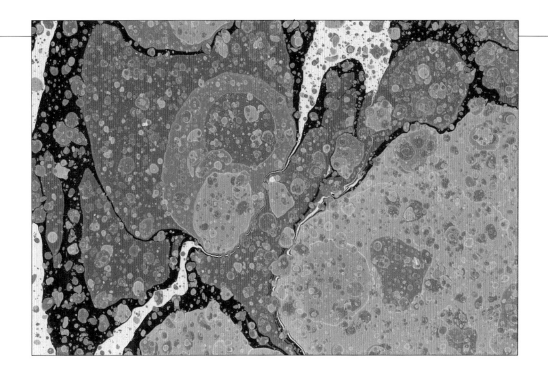

■ BOULDERS WITH SMALL STONES ■

Using a whisk that is loaded fairly heavily with
paint, let large stones fall gently onto the bath.
After laying these boulder-size stones, follow
with a whisk that has only a little paint, tapping
vigorously to make tiny stones.

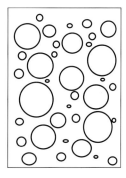

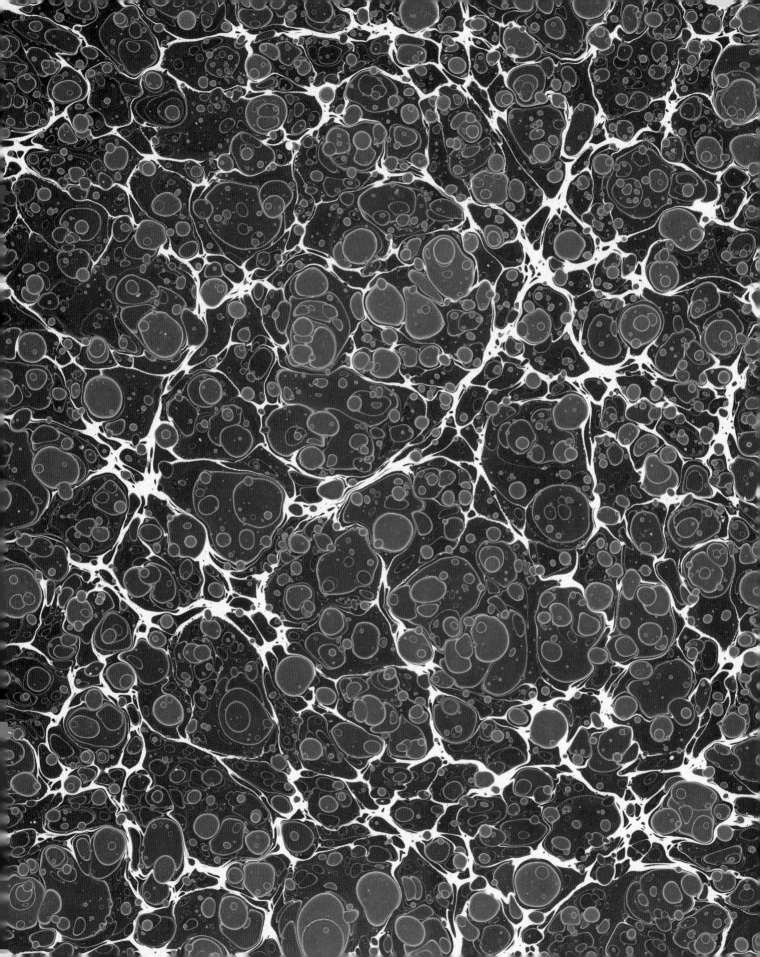

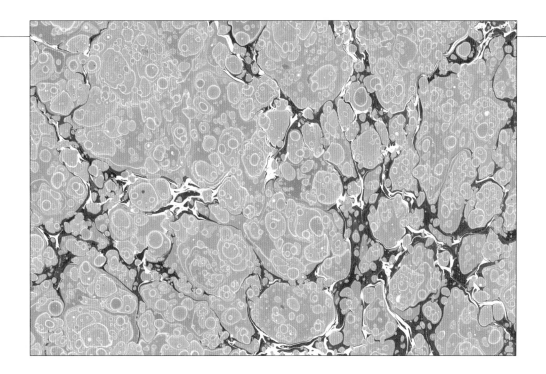

■ S H E L L ■

This pattern stands out because of the white veins and the white halos around each stone. To re-create the large sample at left, quickly cover the surface with an indigo ground color and allow a moment for the drops to expand. Then continue with the same color, but use more force as you tap the whisk. This will produce the white halos around the stones. For the small sample above, use indigo as the ground color, then add stones of terre verte (a gray-green hue).

There is a historical pattern known as French shell, which uses turpentine added to the paint to give the stones a darker center and a very pale edge.

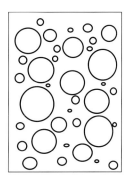

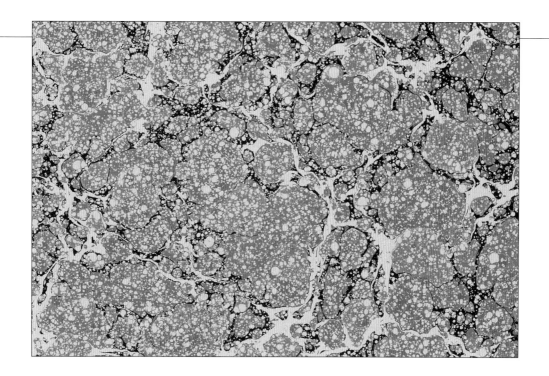

■ SPECKLED STONE ■

Mix a few drops of ox gall with water, and set
the mixture aside for the moment. Make a stone
pattern on the bath, then use an atomizer to spray
a fine mist of gall water over the stones, to produce
the speckled appearance. Indigo is the only color
on the large sample at left. The small sample above
has four colors.

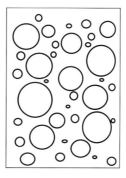

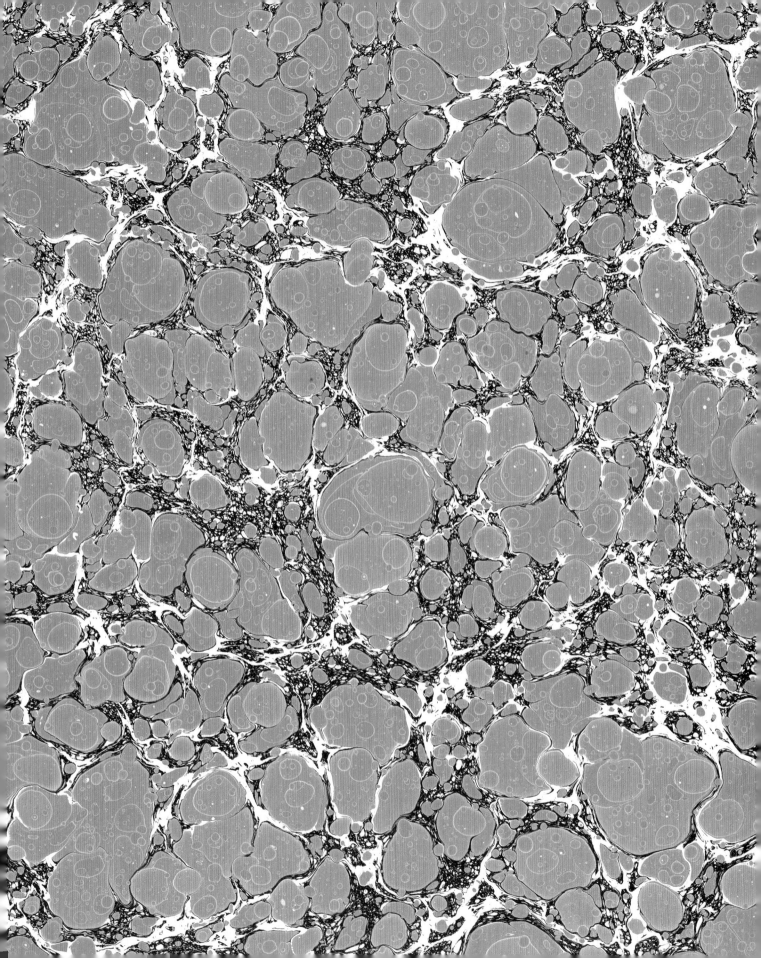

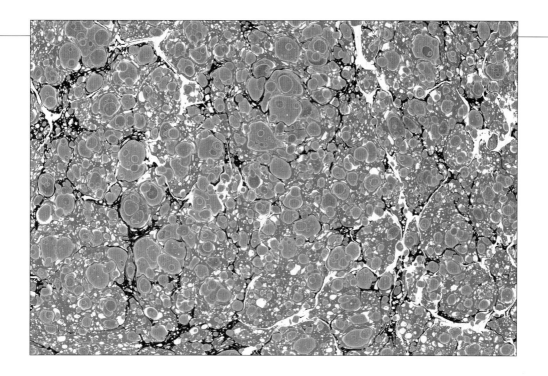

■ SPECKLED STONE VARIATION ■

As for the speckled stone pattern, mix a few drops of ox gall with water and set aside. After applying the ground color, use an atomizer to blow a mist of gall water across the ground color. Then continue to lay additional stones.

For another variation, shown in the small sample above, mist both the indigo ground color and the second color thrown with gall water, then follow with the rust color.

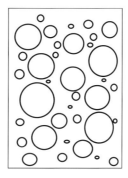

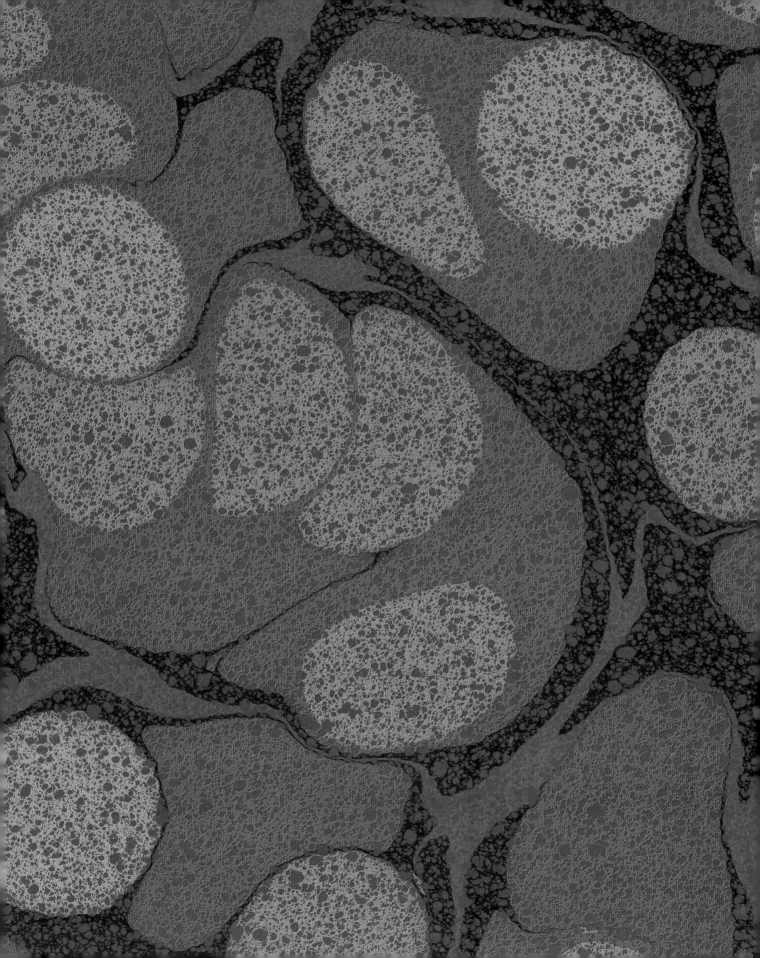

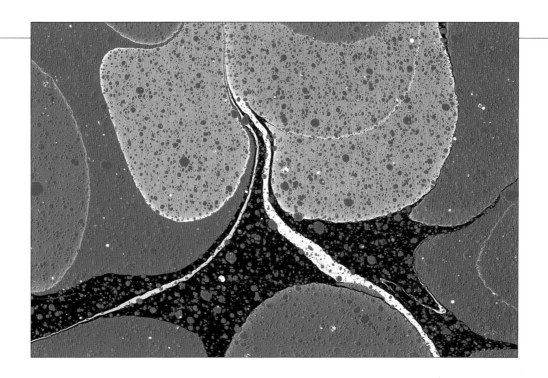

■ SPECKLED ROCK ■

To produce the large stones, adjust the paints with extra drops of ox gall and drop the paints onto the bath with an eye dropper. Then use an atomizer to blow a fine mist of paint across the large stones, or use a toothbrush and flick the paint on with your thumb.

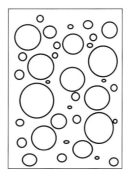

▪ SNAIL ▪

This is a historical pattern popular in France as early as the 1600s. It is also known as French curl. After making a stone pattern, make the snails with a stylus, a rake, or (as in the samples at left and above) with a bouquet comb. The bouquet comb makes two rows of snails at a time and staggers them, as well. Whatever the tool, move the teeth in a circular motion, starting on the outside of the curls and moving to the center. The small sample above was made with a small bouquet comb.

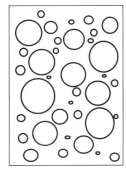

Bouquet Comb

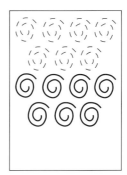

Bouquet Comb

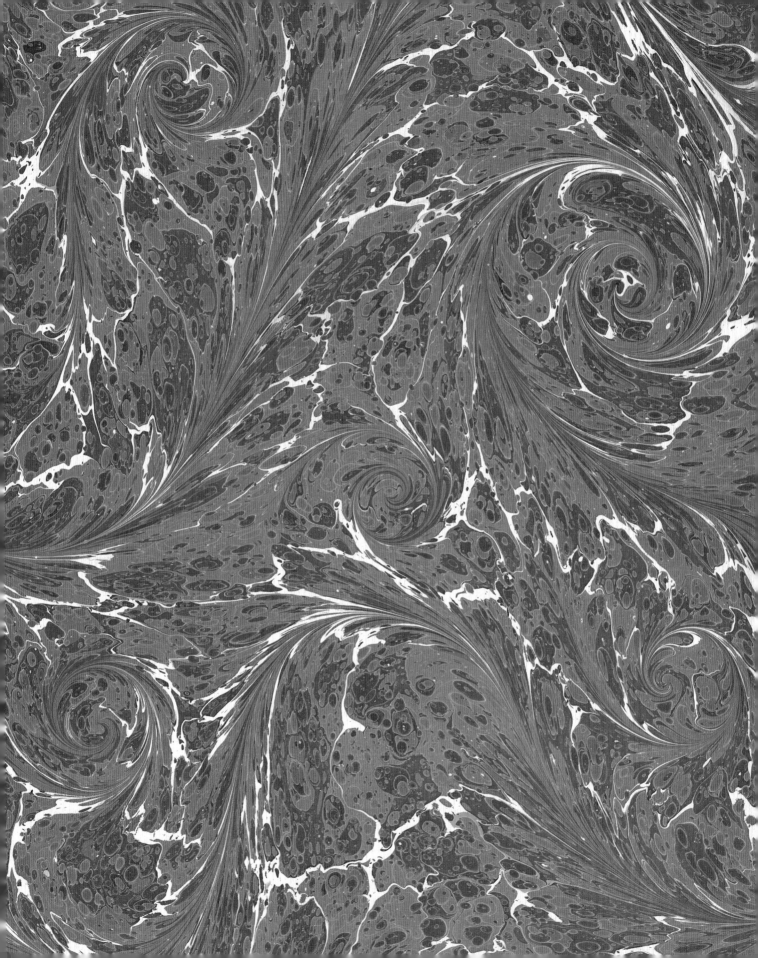

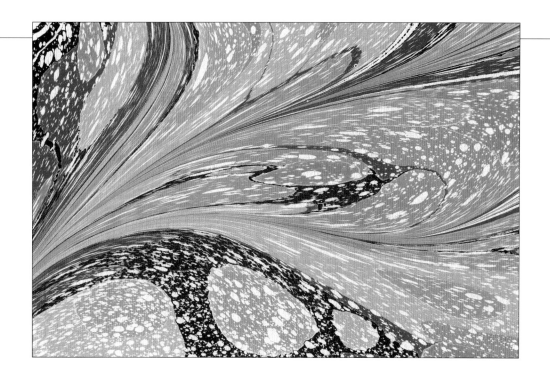

■ DRAWN STONE ■

To make a drawn stone pattern, simply pull a stylus in a freeform motion through the stones. The large sample at left has a few snails added. To make a more regimented pattern, use a rake in a straight or waved motion.

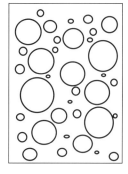
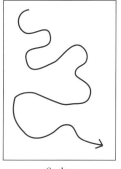

Stylus

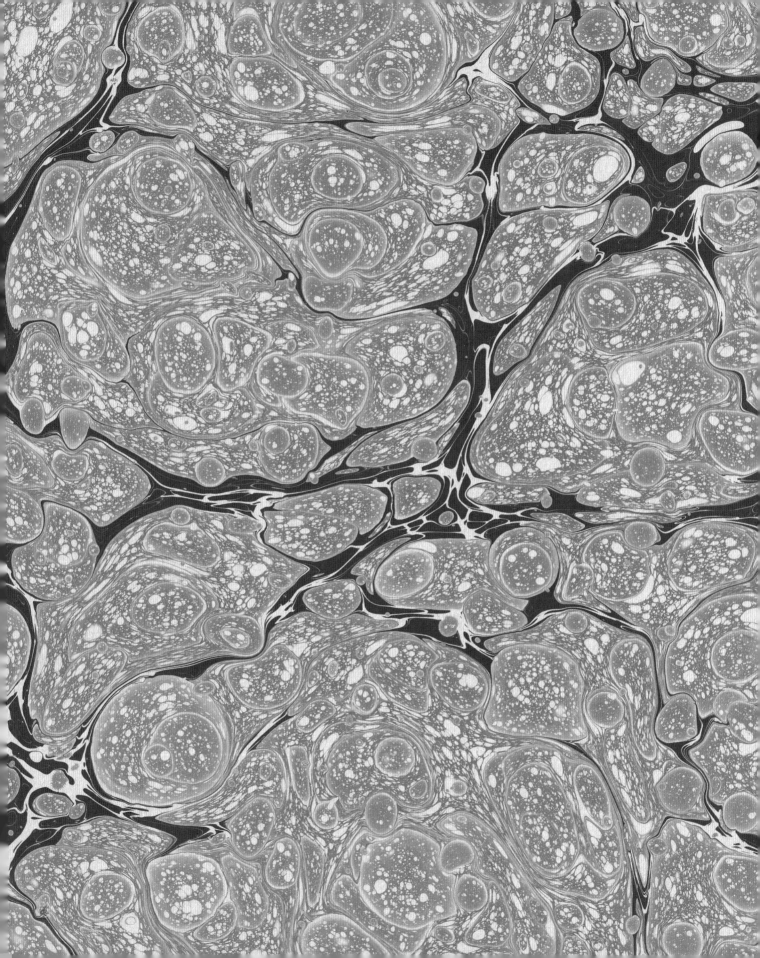

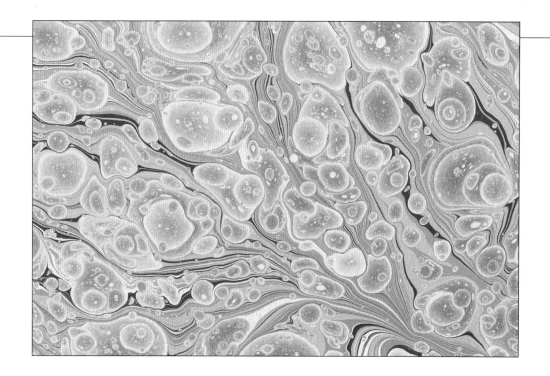

■ STORMONT ■

This pattern is made by adding a drop or two of turpentine to the last color thrown. This causes small holes to open up in the pattern. Be sure not to use the turpentine-paint to make combed patterns, as it will ruin them. No need to dispose of the bath or clean the tank, however. If the weather is dry and hot, any turpentine residue will evaporate from the bath.

When Stormont is done over drawn bands of color—as shown in the small sample above—it is called Gloster.

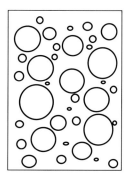

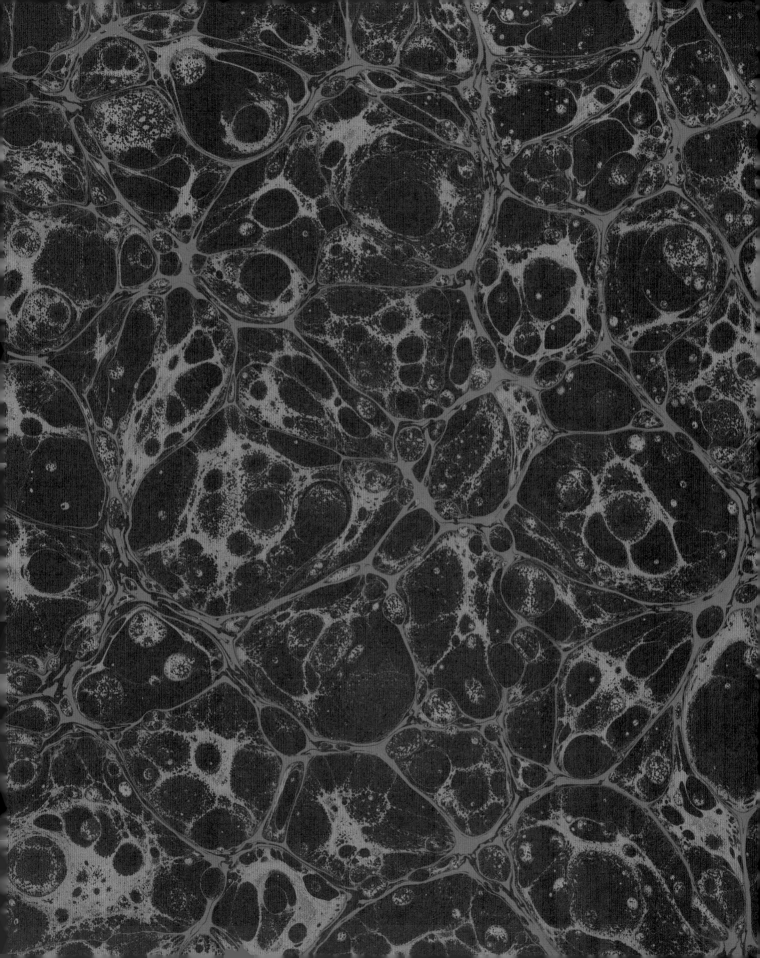

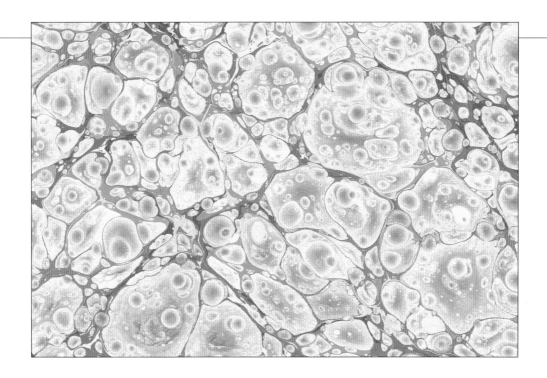

■ OIL SPOT ■

This pattern is made by adding oil to the last color thrown. (Olive oil works well.) Dip a wooden toothpick in the oil, then touch the toothpick to the paint in the jar, so as to add less than one drop. Then throw the paint-oil mixture on a stone pattern, using a whisk. Print quickly, as the tight veins may begin to sink. Once you have made oil spot patterns, throw out the bath and clean the tank with rubbing alcohol and paper towels before doing any combed patterns. Avoid getting the oil-paint mixture on any of your combing tools.

■ ITALIAN HAIR VEIN ■

Begin with a pale stone pattern. Then, using a solution of about one cup (237 ml) water and four drops spirits of soap (or castile liquid soap), sprinkle the solution over the stones. The soap will force the paint into small, tight veins. Print quickly, to avoid the paints sinking. The pattern can also be made with a strong solution of gall water instead of soap.

If soap is used, be sure to keep marbling tools away from it, as it will contaminate them. Use this technique only after you have finished with combed patterns, for any soap residue will interfere with them. Clean up thoroughly.

The large sample at left was made with blue paint on red paper. The small sample above has multiple colors on white paper.

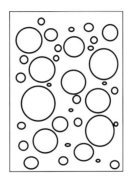

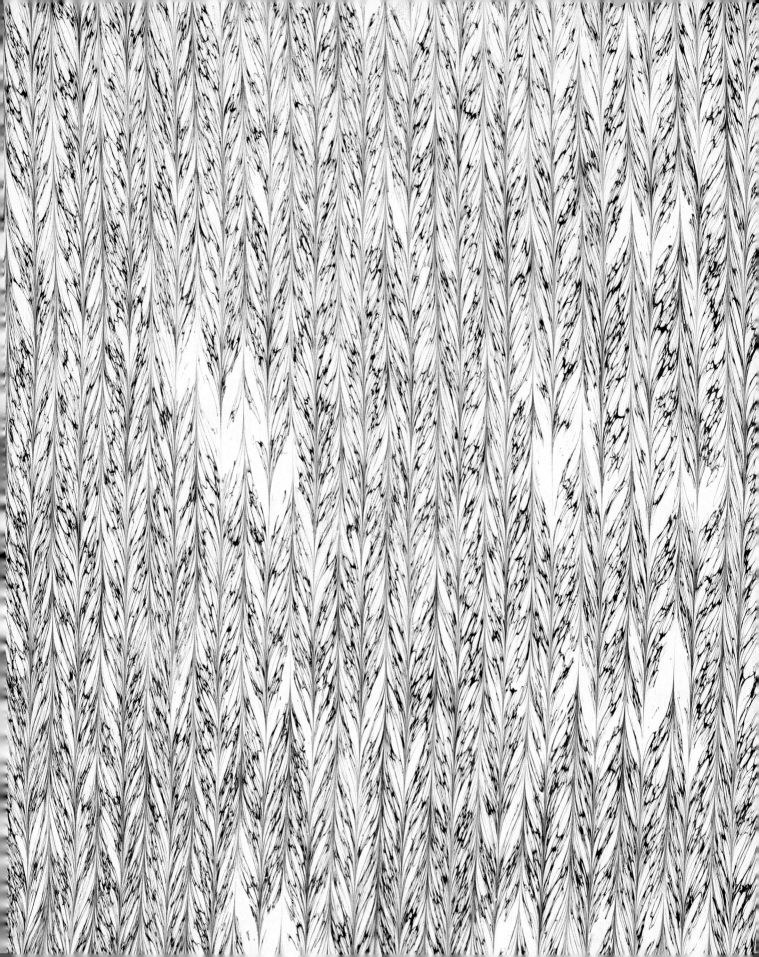

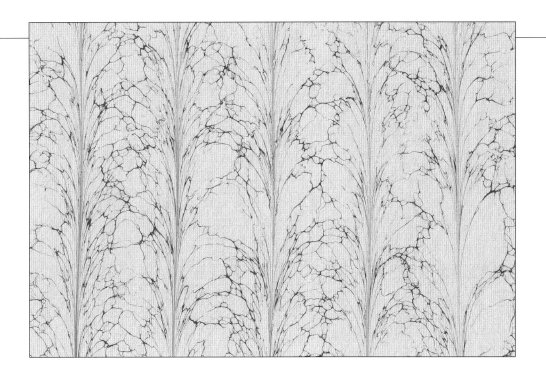

▪ DRAWN ITALIAN HAIR VEIN ▪

To make the large sample shown at left, begin
with an Italian hair vein pattern. Then, using a
1/2" (1 cm) comb, comb up the length of the
tray. Finally, comb back down the tray, bisecting
the first set of lines on the last pass of the comb.
For the small sample above, use a 1" (2.5 cm)
comb to comb down the length of the tray.
Do not comb back up.

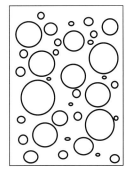

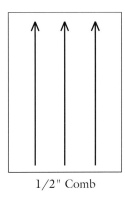

1/2" Comb

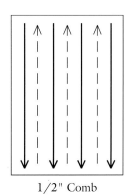

1/2" Comb

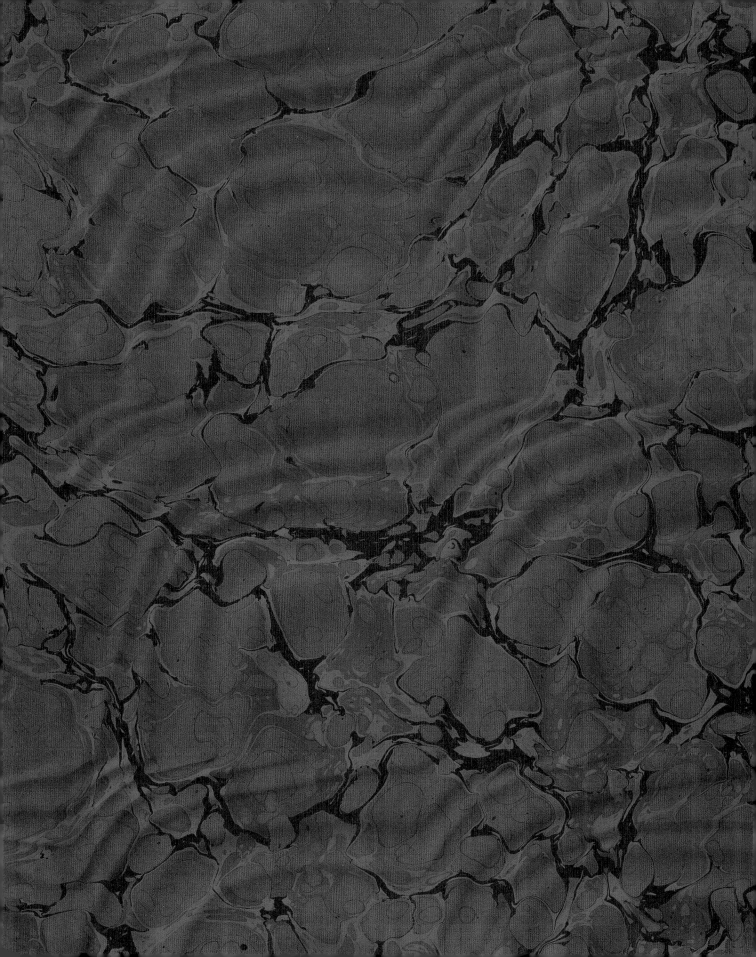

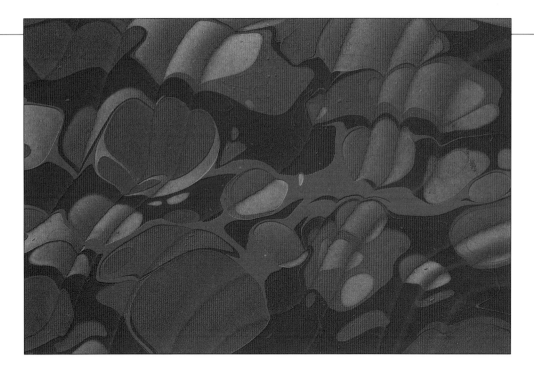

■ MOIRÉ SPANISH ■

This pattern combines a paper-folding and a paper-laying technique to produce the curved lines in the design. As in the samples here, moiré Spanish is traditionally done over a stone pattern, although it can be used on other patterns as well.

To begin, fold the paper into squares. Lay the sheet alumed-side-down on your work surface and roll it up, not too tightly. When it is completely rolled, press it down flat to crease it. (The creases do not have to be very firm.) Now unroll the paper, keeping the alum side down. Turn the paper 1/4 turn and repeat the rolling and flattening process. Open the paper and allow it to relax a few minutes. Your paper should be creased in squares.

The squares on the large sample at left are about 4" (10 cm) in diameter.

Now lay the stone pattern on the bath. To print, hold the paper by diagonally opposite corners. Lay the corner closest to your body on the bath and start a gentle, backward-and-forward motion with your near hand. As you move the paper back and forth, gradually lower it with your far hand, coordinating the movements of both hands until the paper is fully laid on the bath.

This is a difficult maneuver and requires a great deal of practice to master, but the results can be well worth the effort.

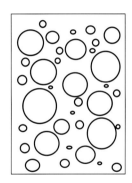

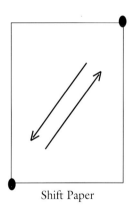

Shift Paper

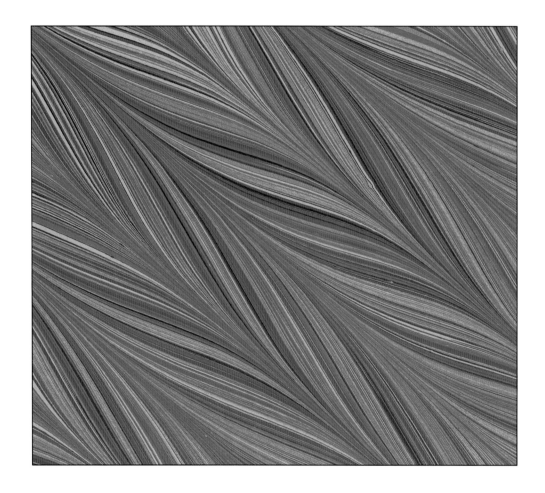

GETGEL

Getgel is a Turkish phrase meaning "go and come," an appropriate name for a pattern that is made by raking across the tray in one direction, then back across in the other. The typical tool is a 2" (5 cm) or 3" (7.5 cm) rake, although a stylus can also be used. The tool should be moved rather quickly, to move the water and stretch the paints into thinner and thinner lines.

Getgel is a bolder pattern than most and often has a more contemporary look, with a texture that is distinctive. Bear in mind that it is the same basic pattern as a chevron, but on a larger scale.

Most combed patterns (for example, nonpareil) begin with a getgel, and most marblers make the pattern twice, one on top of the other, with the second drawn at right angles to the first.

Every time the tools move through the colors on the bath, the color lines are divided and made smaller, becoming more and more delicate. It is possible to do three or more getgels, making each one at right angles to the previous one. For example, if you make a stone pattern with very large stones, you may want to do an extra getgel before combing. If overdone, however, eventually the colors will become muddy and lose their individual identity. Experiment to discover the number of getgels you like best for the combed effects you want.

Determine before you begin whether you want to finish with a horizontal or a vertical getgel. It is a good rule of thumb to have the finished pattern run with the grain of the paper. However, if another pattern will be created on top of the getgel, the final pattern determines the getgel's direction.

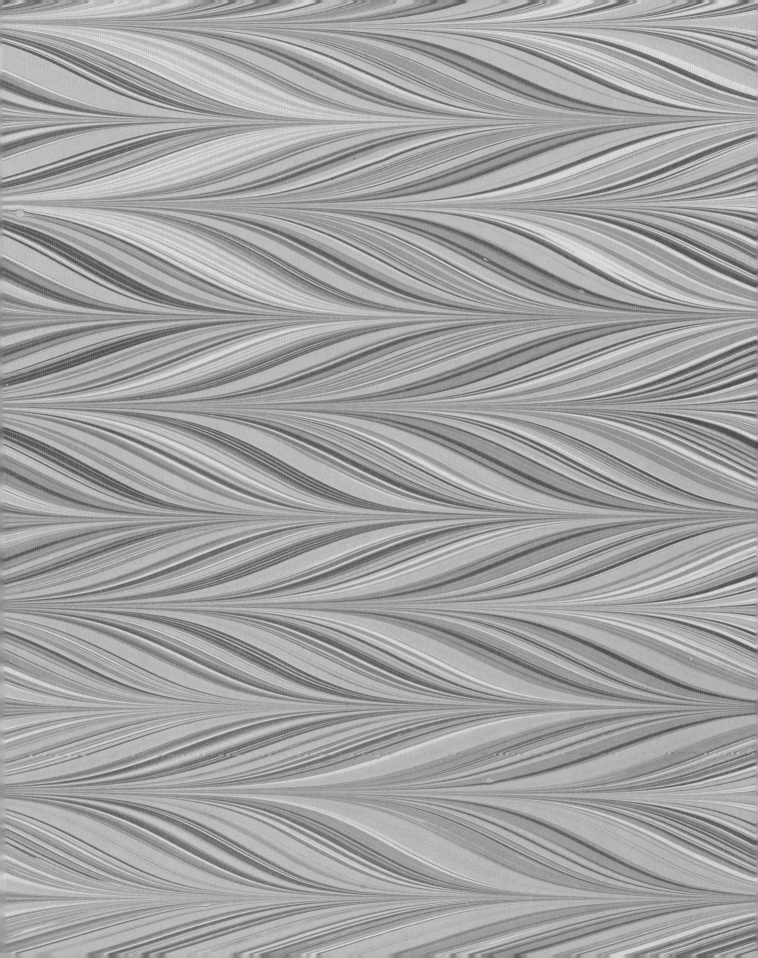

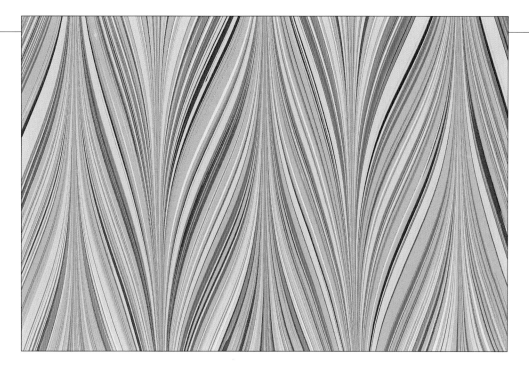

■ G E T G E L ■

The first set of diagrams illustrates a getgel made with a stylus. Starting at a far corner of the tray, draw the stylus toward you across the bath, then draw it away from you, then back toward you, and so on until you've reached the other side of the tray. That is one complete getgel. Now, starting at a far corner of the tray, move the stylus back and forth horizontally, working your way toward yourself until you've covered the surface.

Alternatively, use a rake to make the getgel, as shown in the second set of diagrams.

The large sample at left illustrates a horizontal getgel, made according to the directions above. To make a vertical getgel, as shown in the small

sample, reverse the sequence of movements—that is, first rake back and forth across the bath, then up and down its length. The direction of the last raking determines the direction of the getgel.

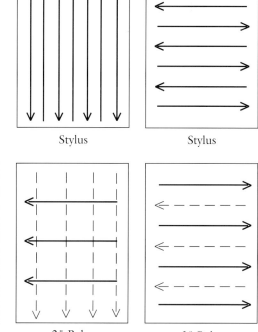

Stylus   Stylus

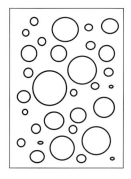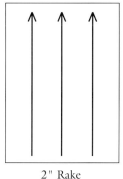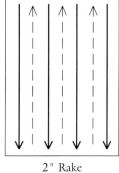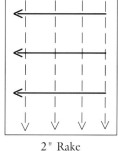

2" Rake   2" Rake   2" Rake   2" Rake

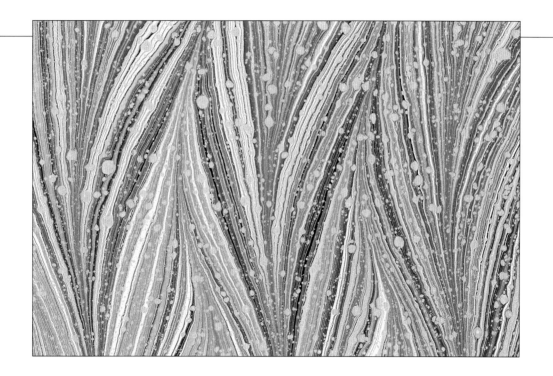

▪ WAVED GETGEL ▪

In making a waved getgel, the last two passes of the pattern must be made with a rake, not a stylus. Make the wave on the last pass of the rake. The large sample at left was made with a 1″ (2.5 cm) rake, as illustrated in the diagrams. The small sample above differs in two respects: it has been "antiqued"—that is, tiny stones were laid on top of the waved getgel—and the last two passes were made with a 2″ (5 cm) rake.

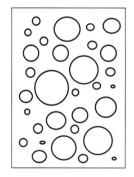

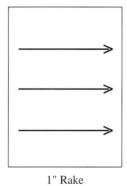

1″ Rake

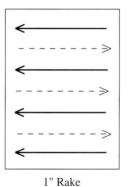

1″ Rake

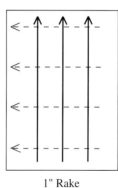

1″ Rake

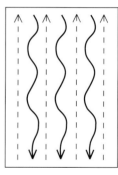

1″ Rake

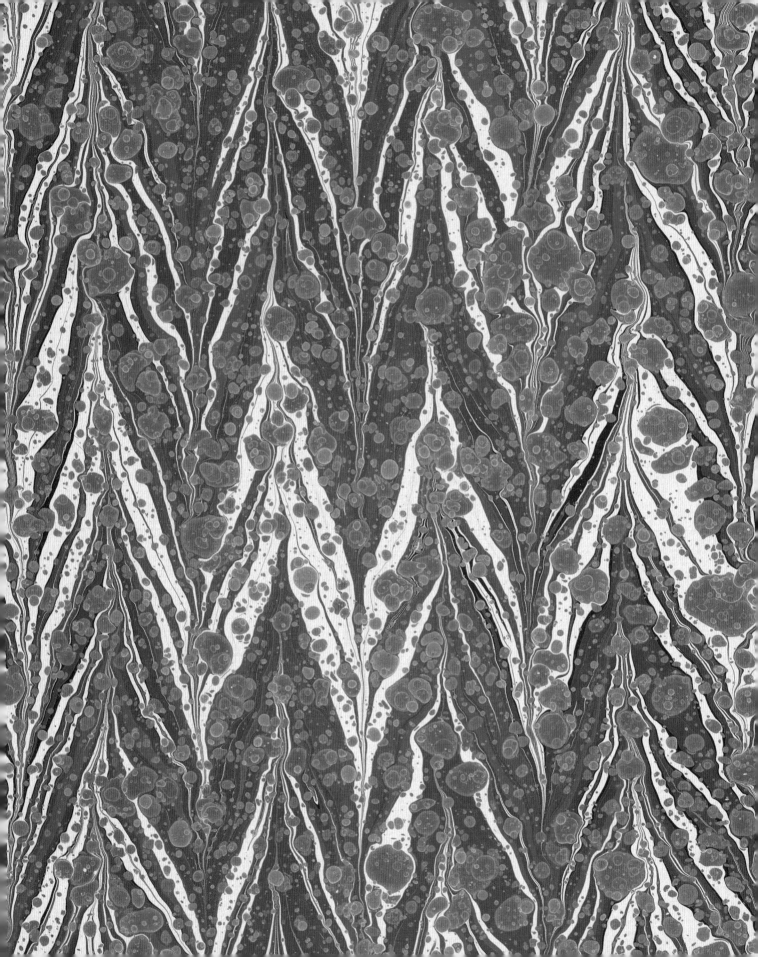

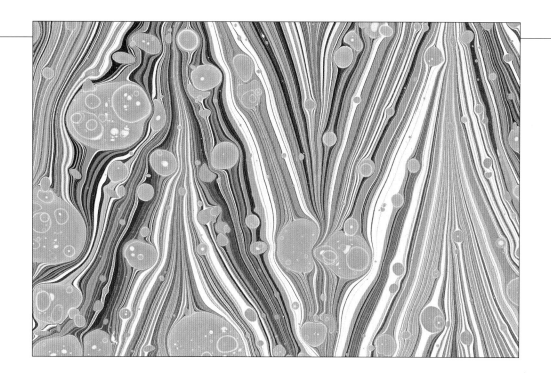

■ ZEBRA ■

A zebra pattern (also known as an antiqued getgel) is a standard getgel with stones on top. The stones push against the lines of paint, moving them out of alignment. The large sample at left, made with a 2" (5 cm) rake, has stones of two colors. The small sample above was made with a 3" (7.5 cm) rake.

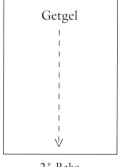

Getgel

2" Rake

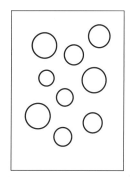

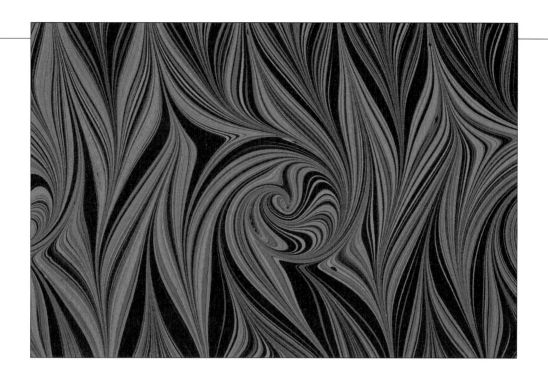

▪ GETGEL CURL ▪

For the large sample at left, make a vertical getgel
with a 3" (7.5 cm) rake. Then place the teeth of the
rake along one of the drawn lines in the getgel and
make the curls, moving from the outside of the
curls to their centers. Space the next row of curls by
skipping one or two of the pattern lines, then repeat
the curling motion. For the small sample above, use
a 1" (2.5 cm) rake to make the vertical getgel and a
stylus to make the curls.

Getgel

3" Rake

3" Rake

3" Rake

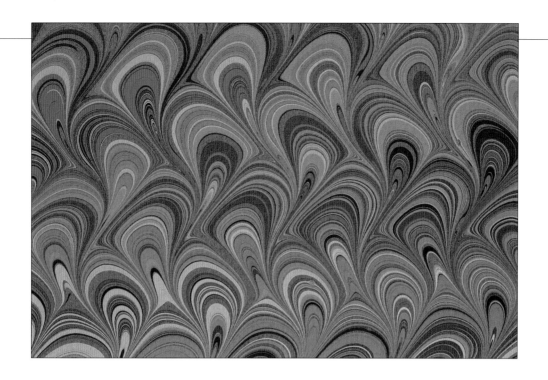

▪ PEACOCK ▪

Begin with a horizontal getgel made with a 2"
(5 cm) rake. Pull the bouquet comb through the
lines in a controlled wave. Learning to use a bouquet comb takes practice, as the forward movement
must be coordinated with the sideways motion to
make an oval figure. The small sample above was
made with a small bouquet comb.

Getgel

2" Rake

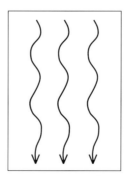

Bouquet Comb

■ CABLED GETGEL ■

To make the large sample at left, begin with a vertical getgel made with a 2" (5 cm) rake. Then, using a 3" (7.5 cm) rake, move horizontally from left to right. Shift the rake up 1/2" (1 cm) and rake back from right to left, forming the cable.

To make the small sample above, follow the same procedure, but use a 1" (2.5 cm) rake to make the getgel and a 1-1/2" (4 cm) comb to cable it.

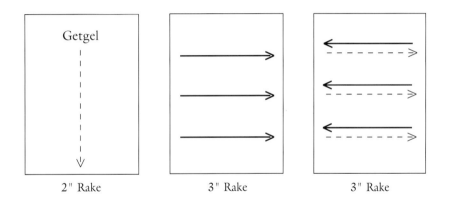

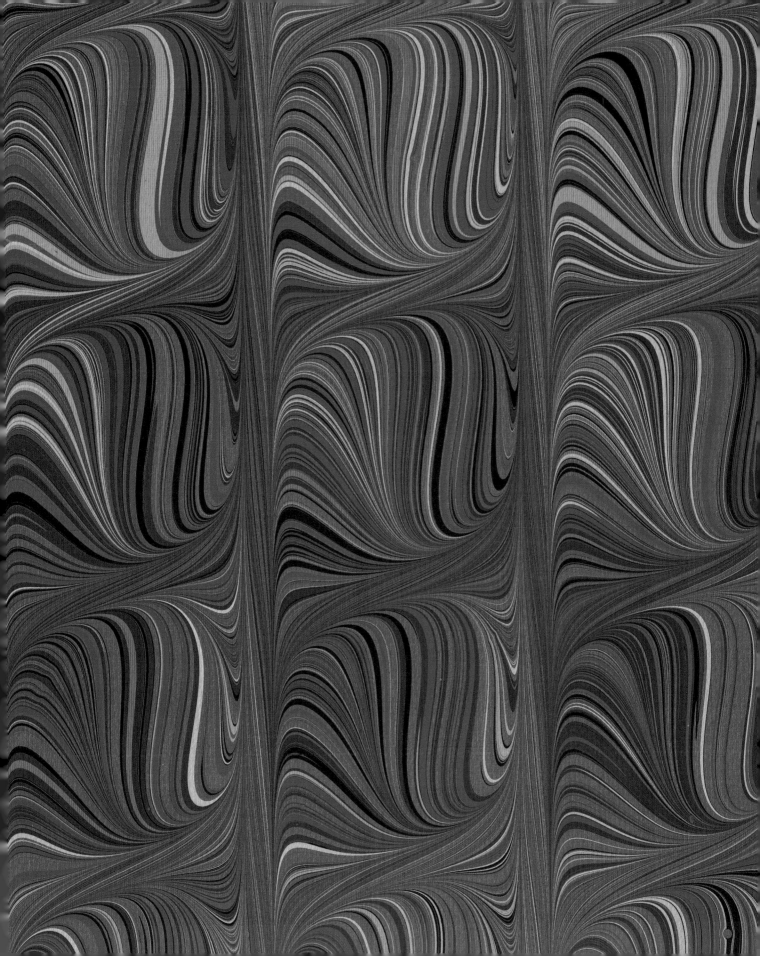

▪ DOUBLE CABLED GETGEL ▪

To make the large pattern shown at left, begin
with a vertical getgel made with a 3" (7.5 cm) rake.
Follow the instructions for a cabled getgel on the
previous pages, completing a horizontal cable.
Then cable again, this time vertically. To make the
small sample shown above, follow the same procedure, but use a 2" (5 cm) rake.

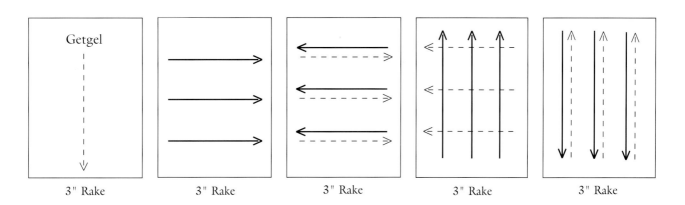

Getgel

3" Rake   3" Rake   3" Rake   3" Rake   3" Rake

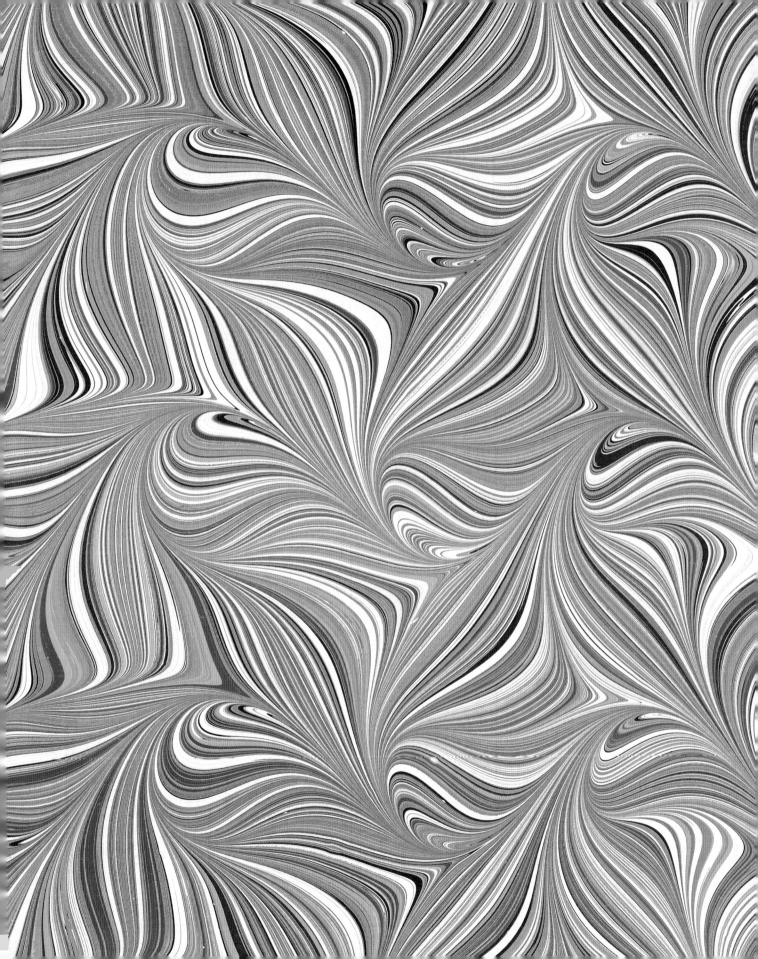

■ ANGEL FISH ■

Reminiscent of the work of artist M. C. Escher, this pattern begins with a vertical getgel made with a 3″ (7.5 cm) rake. To complete the pattern, draw the 3″ rake horizontally in a rhythmic wave. Return in a similar motion, crossing the first wave and creating a series of horizontal figure eights. This pattern can be varied by creating shallow or deep waves. The small sample above was made with a 2″ (5 cm) rake.

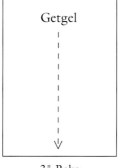

3″ Rake

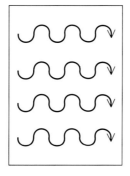

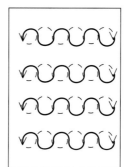

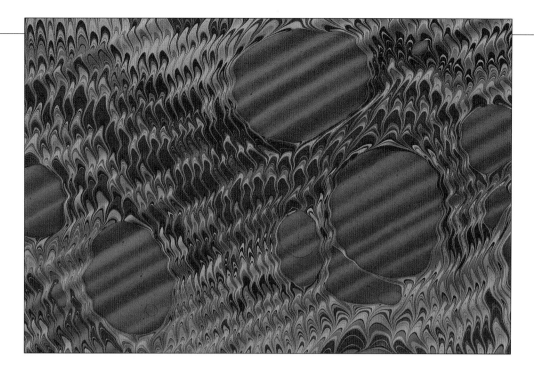

■ SPANISH ■

The term *Spanish* refers to a paper-laying technique, which can be used with various patterns. To make the large sample at left, begin with a vertical getgel. When you are ready to print, hold the paper diagonally, by opposite corners. Lay the corner closest to you on the bath and start a gentle, backward-and-forward motion with that hand. As you move the paper back and forth, gradually lower it with your other hand, coordinating the movements of both hands until the paper is fully laid on the bath. Small papers are easier to work with, especially at first.

The small sample above illustrates the Spanish technique applied to a nonpareil pattern (see page 69) with some stones added on top of it.

This paper-shifting, rock-and-drag technique is attributed to a Spanish marbler who, having overindulged the night before, transferred his shakiness to the paper as he marbled. His employer received the mistake with enthusiasm and asked him to perfect the technique

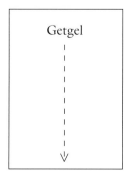

Getgel

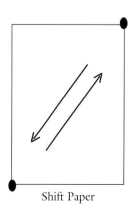

Shift Paper

▪ NEW JERSEY RIPPLE ▪

Iris Nevins contributed—and named—this variation of a Spanish moiré. Start by folding the paper. If you work with dry, pre-alumed paper, lay the sheet alumed-side-down on your work surface. Roll up the paper, not too tightly. When it is completely rolled, rub it down flat to crease it. (The creases do not have to be very hard.) Now unroll the paper, keeping the alum side down. Give the sheet 1/4 turn and repeat the rolling and flattening process. Open the paper and allow it to relax a few minutes. Your paper should be creased in squares. The squares on the large sample at left are about 4" (10 cm) in diameter.

If you prefer to work on dampened paper, draw the design on the bath before you fold the paper. If you like, antique it by adding small drops of paint or gall water. Roll the sheet as described above, then lay it under a board for about 10 seconds to make it more manageable.

Lay the paper onto the bath with the same back-and-forth motion described on page 63 for Spanish. The creases in the paper will cause the lines created by the Spanish technique to curve (moiré) across the paper.

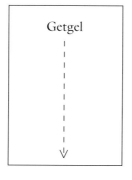

Getgel

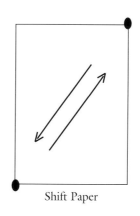

Shift Paper

NONPAREIL

Throughout the world this pattern bears the name the French gave it. *Nonpareil* means "without equal" and has been so popular in French marbling since at least the 17th century that its other name is "French marble."

Nonpareil is a base pattern for a whole series of other patterns created by moving rakes and/or combs over the nonpareil. Some of these are the most popular present-day patterns, such as bouquet. This section demonstrates the incredible variety of patterns that can be made by changing the size of combs and rakes, the sequence of their use, and the direction of movement. It also illustrates how scale can change the effect of a pattern so that patterns can be designed for specific uses. Many of the patterns in this section are compound patterns—for example, a getgel over a nonpareil to make a feather pattern, thus creating a new pattern language.

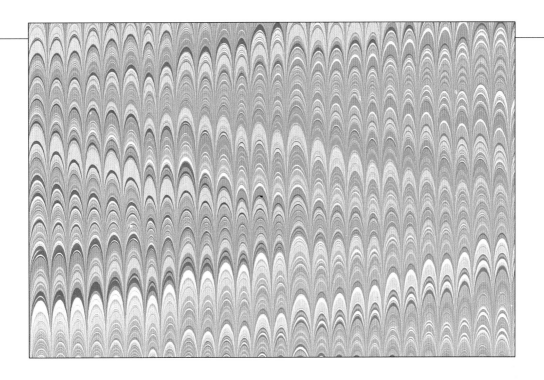

■ NONPAREIL ■

Begin with a horizonal getgel. Comb through it vertically. The large sample at left was made with a 1/8" (3 mm) comb. The small sample above was made with a 1/4" (6 mm) comb.

If the comb used is 1/2" (1 cm) or larger, the pattern is called cascade.

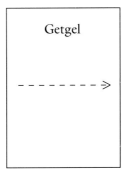

Getgel

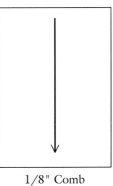

1/8" Comb

■ WAVED NONPAREIL ■

Make a vertical nonpareil. Then rake vertically down the tray in a wavy, side-to-side motion. Variations can be created by increasing or decreasing the sideways motion and by using different sizes of tools for both the nonpareil and the wave. The large sample at left was made by using a 3" (7.5 cm) rake to wave a 1/8" (3 mm) nonpareil. The small sample above consists of a 1" (2.5 cm) rake over a 1/8" nonpareil. (If this waved movement is made over a horizontal getgel, it makes a pattern known as pillow.)

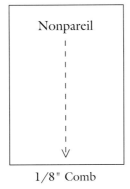

1/8" Comb

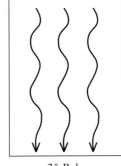

3" Rake

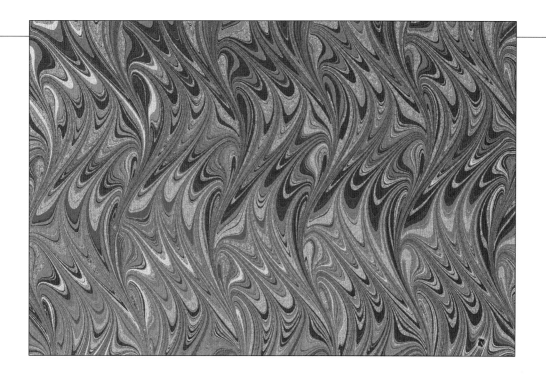

▪ R E V E R S E   W A V E ▪

Reverse wave is identical to a waved nonpareil except that the final raking movement is upward, raking against the nonpareil instead of with it. After the paper is printed, turn it upside down (top to bottom) to display the finished pattern.

The large sample at left illustrates a 3″ (7.5 cm) rake over a 1/8″ (3 mm) nonpareil. The small sample above illustrates a 1″ (2.5 cm) rake over a 1/4″ (6 mm) nonpareil.

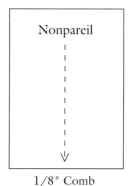

1/8″ Comb

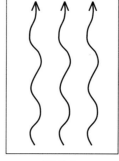

3″ Rake

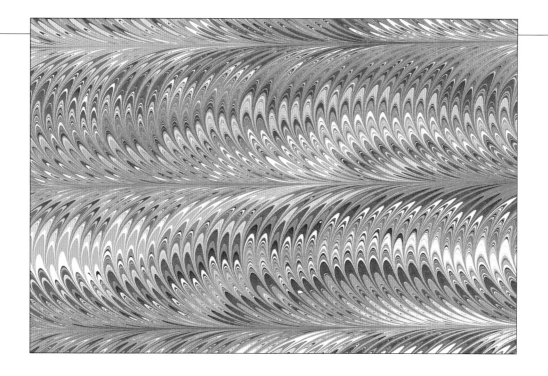

■ ICARUS ■

For the large sample at left, begin by making a vertical nonpareil, using a 1/8" (3 mm) comb. Then rake across it horizontally with a 2" (5 cm) rake. For the small sample above, comb the nonpareil horizontally with a 1-1/2" (4 cm) comb, instead. This pattern is also known as small Dutch or, if made with larger combs and rakes, large Dutch.

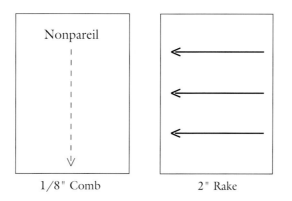

Nonpareil

1/8" Comb   2" Rake

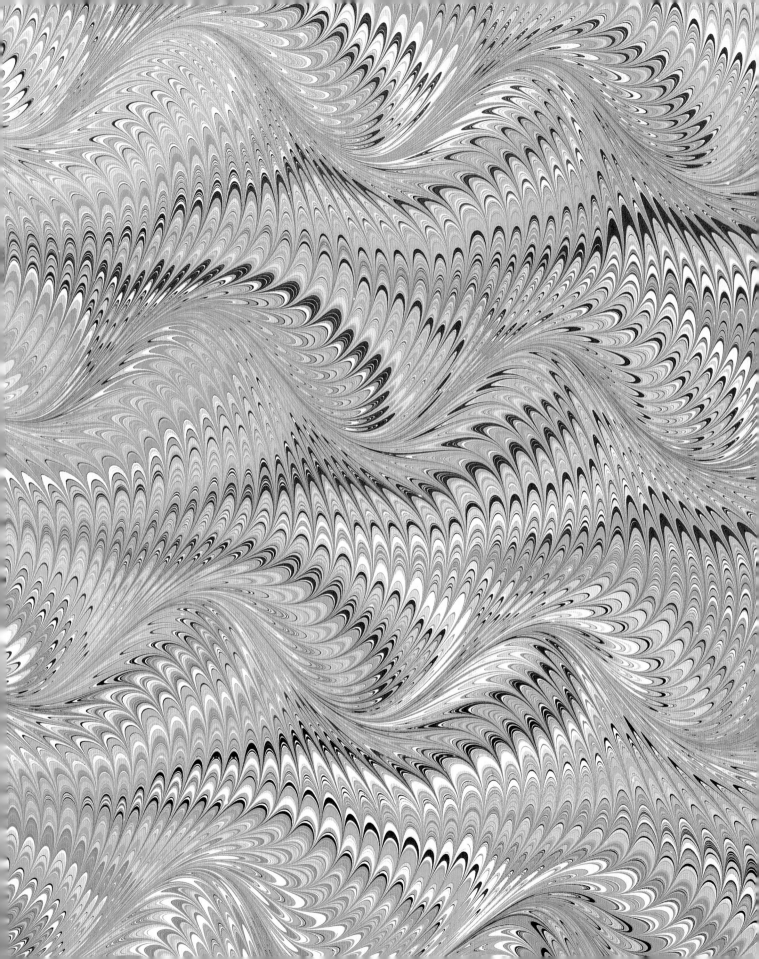

▪ WAVED ICARUS ▪

To make the large sample at left, start with a vertical nonpareil made with a 1/4" (6 mm) comb. Move across it horizontally with a 3" (7.5 cm) rake, using a gentle, sweeping, serpentine motion. For a very different result, try moving in a quick wiggle instead.

The small sample above was made by waving with a 1-1/2" (4 cm) comb over a 1/8" (3 mm) nonpareil.

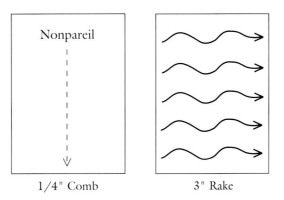

Nonpareil

1/4" Comb   3" Rake

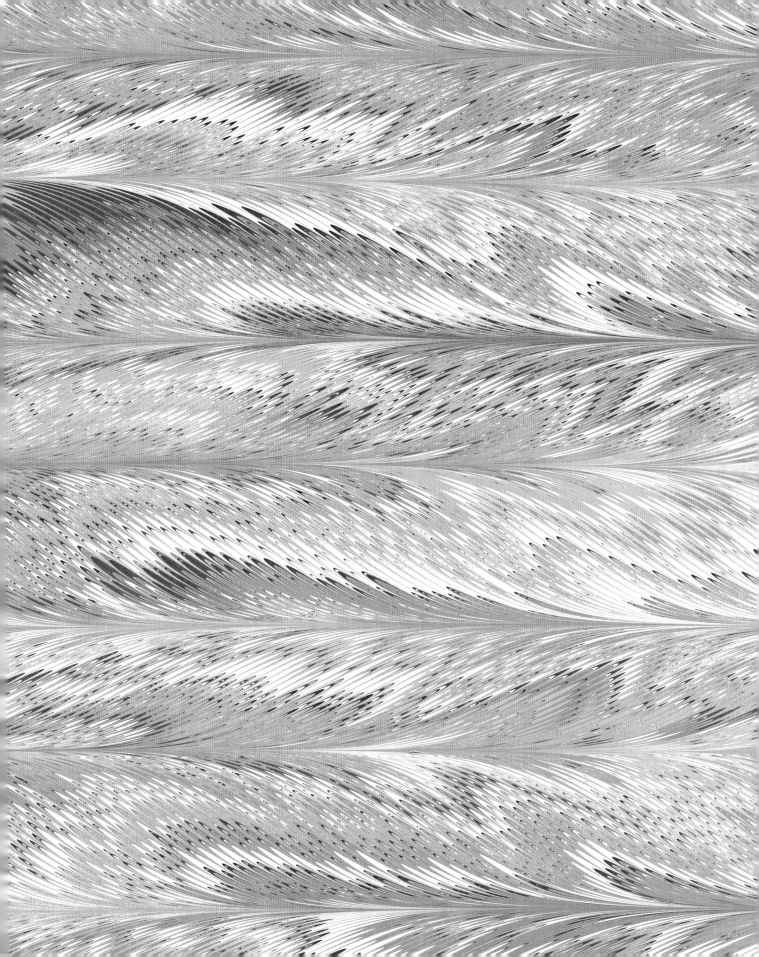

■ FEATHER ■

First create a vertical nonpareil, using a 1/8"
(3 mm) comb. Then rake back and forth across it,
using a 3" (7.5 cm) rake. Basically, this pattern is
a getgel across a nonpareil. For the small sample,
use a 1/4" (6 mm) comb for the nonpareil and
a 1-1/2" (4 cm) comb across it.

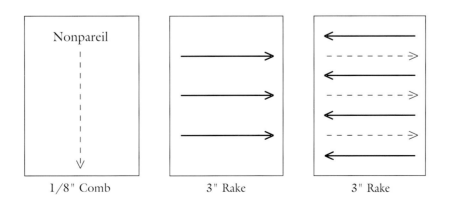

Nonpareil

1/8" Comb   3" Rake   3" Rake

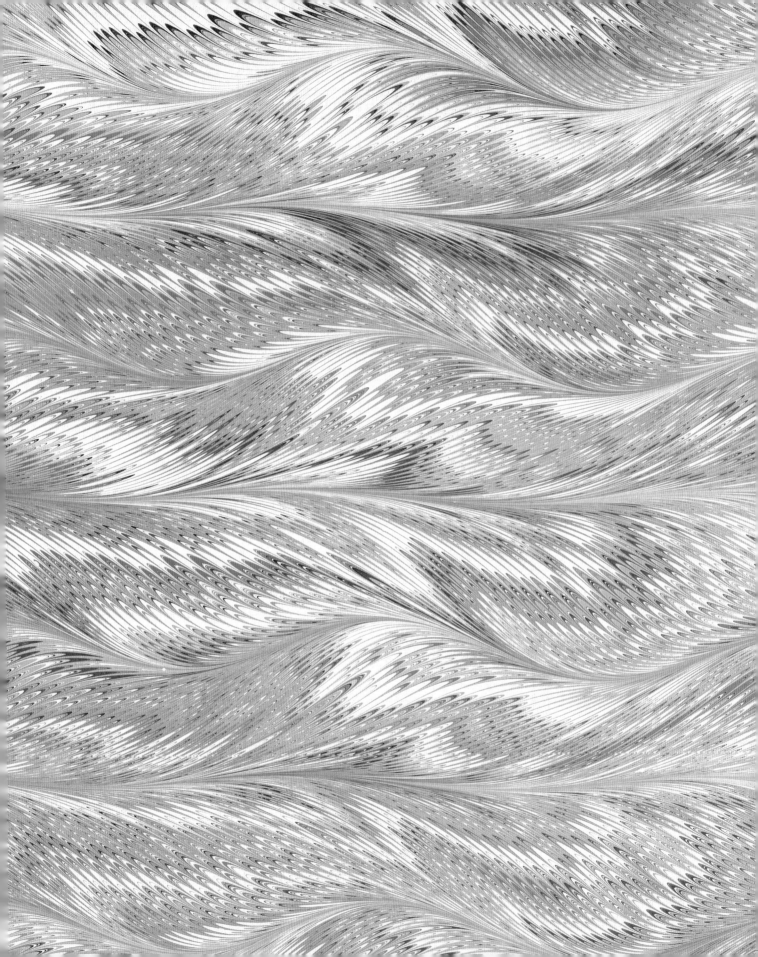

■ FEATHER WAVE ■

Make a vertical nonpareil, using a 1/8" (3 mm) comb. Then proceed to make a waved getgel across it: rake across the bath with a 3" (7.5 cm) rake, then rake back across in the other direction with a wavy, serpentine motion. For the small sample, use a 1/8" (3 mm) comb for the nonpareil and a 1-1/2" (4 cm) comb across it.

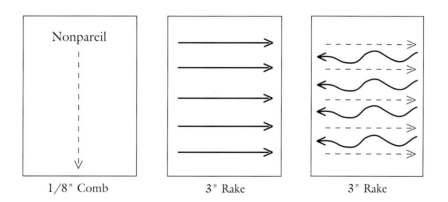

Nonpareil

1/8" Comb

3" Rake

3" Rake

■ F O U N T A I N ■

For the large sample at left, begin with a vertical
nonpareil made with a 1/8" (3 mm) comb. Rake
back and forth across it with a 3" (7.5 cm) rake,
to create the feather pattern. Then rake vertically
down the tray with the 3" rake, to complete the
fountain pattern.

Scale changes the look of this pattern dramati-
cally. The small sample above is a 1/4" (6 mm)
nonpareil manipulated with a 1-1/2" (4 cm) comb.

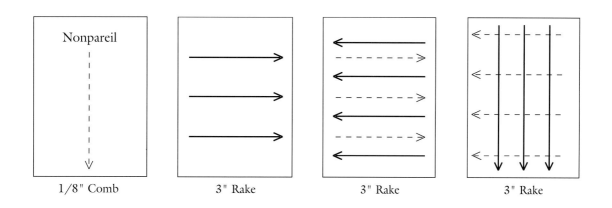

1/8" Comb   3" Rake   3" Rake   3" Rake

■ BOUQUET ■

After making a vertical nonpareil, move down the tray from top to bottom with a bouquet comb, using a controlled, sideways wave. Pattern sizes vary with the size of the tools. The large sample at left was made with a large bouquet comb over a 1/8" (3 mm) nonpareil. The small sample above was made with a 1/4" (6 mm) nonpareil and a small bouquet comb.

If the bouquet comb is used in this fashion on an uncombed getgel, a peacock pattern results.

Nonpareil

1/8" Comb

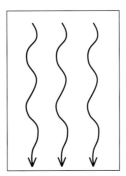

Bouquet Comb

■ REVERSE BOUQUET ■

Begin with a vertical nonpareil made with a 1/8″ (3 mm) comb. Using the bouquet comb, move from the bottom of the tray to the top, using a wavy motion. This simply reverses the direction of the final combing of the bouquet pattern. The small sample above was made with a smaller bouquet comb.

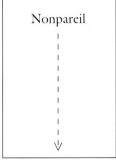

Nonpareil

1/8″ Comb

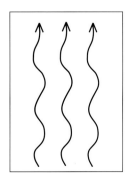

Bouquet Comb

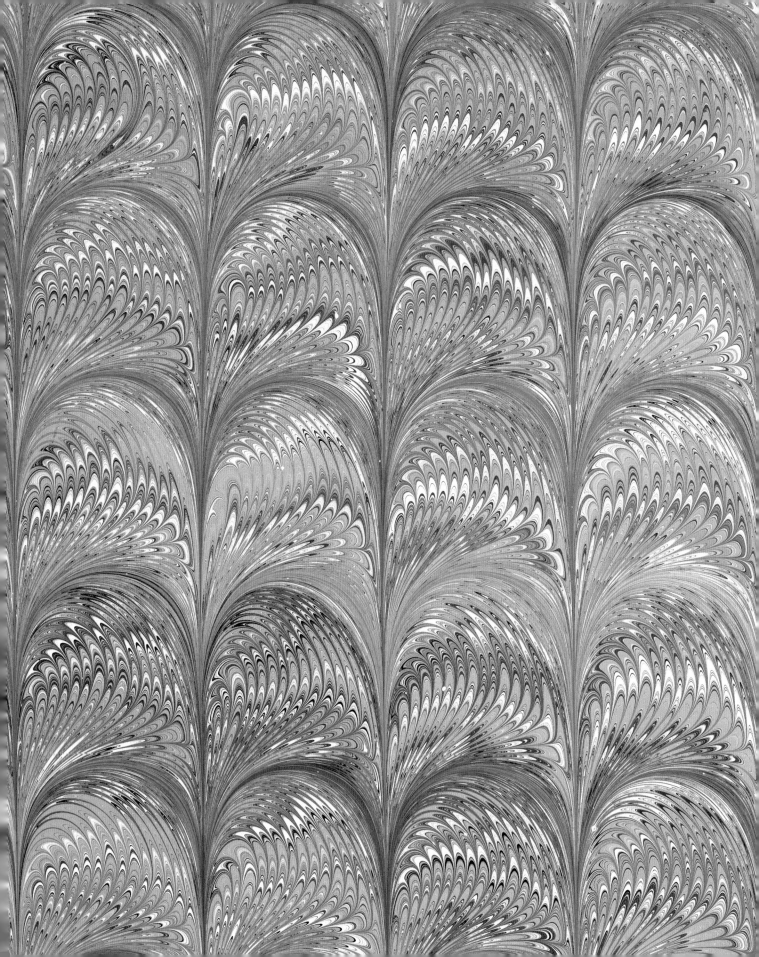

■ CATHEDRAL ■

First make a vertical nonpareil, using a 1/8"
(3 mm) comb. Then move across it horizontally
with a 2" (5 cm) rake. Finally, rake from top to
bottom with the 2" rake. For the small sample,
again make a 1/8" nonpareil but use a 1" (2.5 cm)
comb for the additional steps.

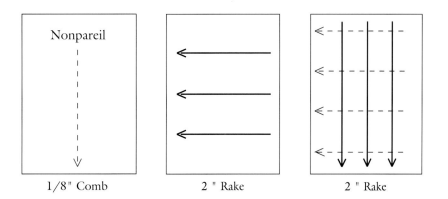

Nonpareil		
1/8" Comb	2 " Rake	2 " Rake

▪ F A U X   B O U Q U E T ▪

We named this pattern faux (or false) bouquet because it strongly resembles a true bouquet. The directions for this pattern are the same as those for cathedral, except that the last movement is waved. Start with a vertical nonpareil made with a 1/8" (3 mm) comb. Rake across the nonpareil with a 2" (5 cm) rake, then rake down the length of the tray in a gentle, wavy motion.

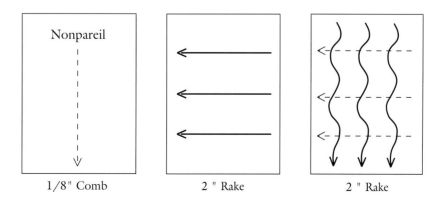

1/8" Comb   2 " Rake   2 " Rake

■ SCALLOP ■

First make a vertical nonpareil, using either a 1/8"
(3 mm) comb, as in the large sample at left, or a
1/4" (6 mm) comb, as in the small sample above.
Then use the bouquet comb horizontally, moving
across the bath in a wavy motion.

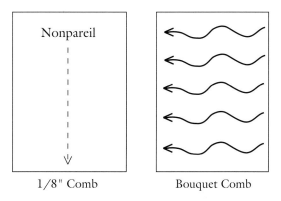

Nonpareil

1/8" Comb   Bouquet Comb

■ FRENCH CURL ■

This historic pattern is also called snail. To make it, begin with a vertical nonpareil made with a 1/8" (3 mm) comb. Using a 3" (7.5 cm) rake, form the curls, moving from the outside to the center of each curl. Stagger the curls in the next row. Curls can also be made with a bouquet comb, which makes two rows at a time and automatically staggers the curls.

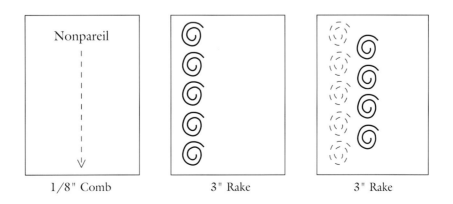

Nonpareil

1/8" Comb   3" Rake   3" Rake

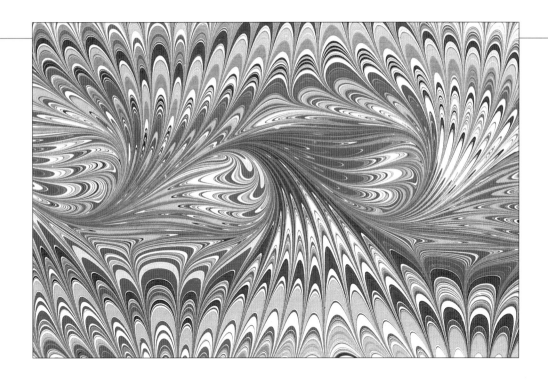

■ ANGEL'S WING ■

Make a vertical nonpareil, using either a 1/8"
(3 mm) comb, as in the large sample at left, or a
1/4" (6 mm) comb, as in the small sample above.
Then rake horizontally with a 3" (7.5 cm) rake,
moving from left to right in a rhythmic wave.
Finally, rake from right to left with the same
undulating motion, crossing over the first waves
and making a series of horizontal figure eights.

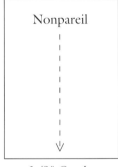

1/8" Comb

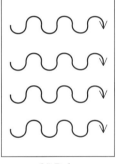

3" Rake

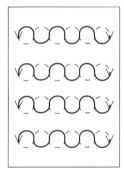

3" Rake

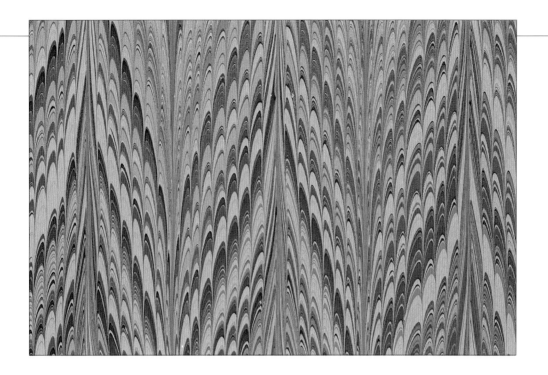

▪ G O T H I C ▪

Begin with a vertical nonpareil made with a 1/8″ (3 mm) comb. Rake up the tray from bottom to top with a 3″ (7.5 cm) rake. Position the rake so that the teeth bisect the lines of the previous stroke, and rake down from top to bottom. (The small sample above was made with a 2″ [5 cm] rake.) This pattern is a vertical getgel over a vertical nonpareil.

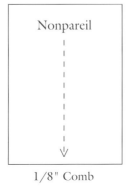

1/8″ Comb

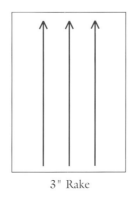

3″ Rake

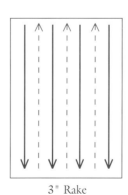

3″ Rake

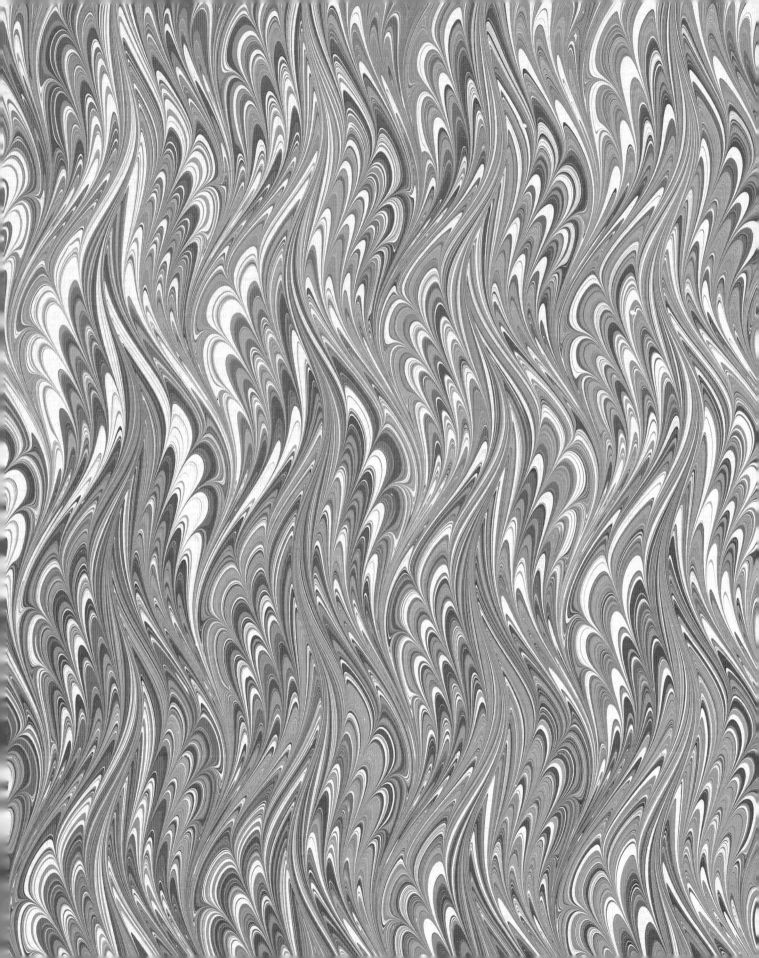

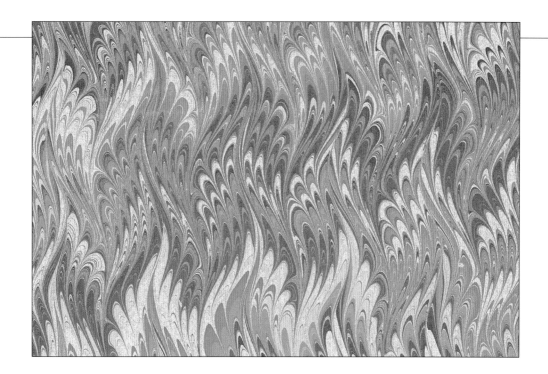

■ WAVED GOTHIC ■

For the large sample at left, first make a vertical
nonpareil, using a 1/4" (6 mm) comb. Rake up
the length of the tray with a 2" (5 cm) rake. Then,
bisecting the lines of the last stroke, rake down the
tray in a wavy motion. (This is the same movement
as a waved getgel.) For the small sample, use a
1/8" (3 mm) nonpareil and add the waved getgel
with a 1" (2.5 cm) comb.

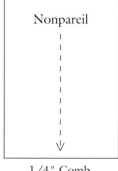

1/4" Comb

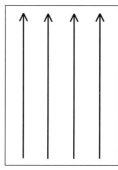

2" Rake

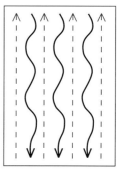

2" Rake

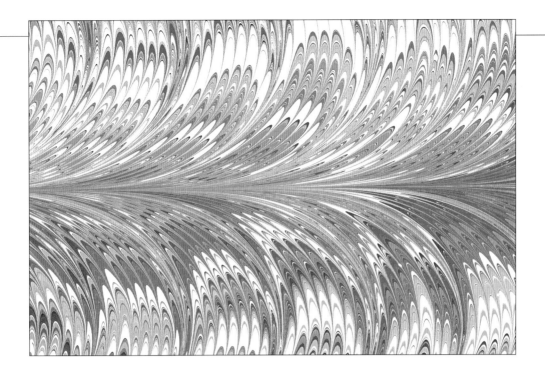

▪ ICARUS VARIATION ▪

After making a 1/8" (3 mm) vertical nonpareil, rake down from top to bottom, using a 1" (2.5 cm) rake. Then comb horizontally from right to left, using either a 1-1/2" (4 cm) comb, as in the large sample, or a 3" (7.5 cm) rake, as in the small sample.

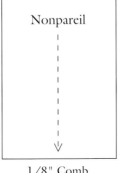

1/8" Comb

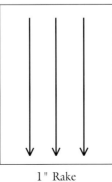

1" Rake

1-1/2" Comb

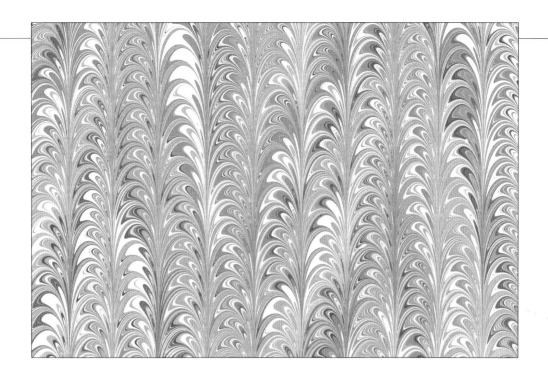

■ AMERICAN ■

For the large sample at left, begin with a horizontal nonpareil made with a 3/8" (1 cm) comb. Then comb vertically from top to bottom with a 1/4" (6 mm) comb. To make the small sample above, again make a 3/8" vertical nonpareil, but comb from top to bottom with a 1/2" (1 cm) comb. This pattern, also called American feather, is traditionally made using the same size comb both vertically and horizontally.

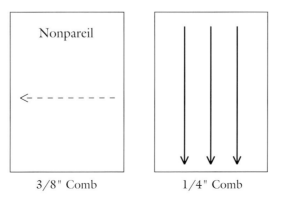

Nonpareil

3/8" Comb   1/4" Comb

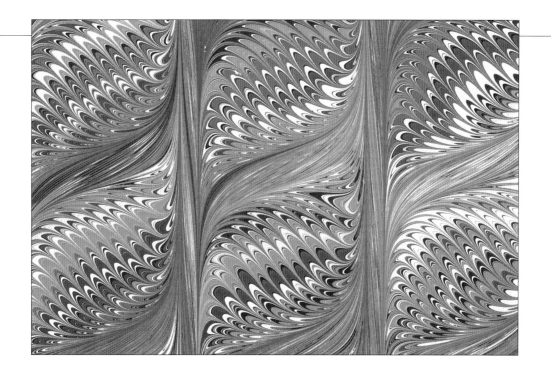

■ DOUBLE CABLED NONPAREIL ■

Start with a vertical nonpareil—either a 1/4"
(6 mm) one, as in the large sample at left, or a
1/8" (3 mm) one, as in the small sample above.
In either case, comb horizontally from left to right
with a 1-1/2" (3 cm) comb. Move the comb up
1/4" and comb back from right to left, forming a
cable. Now comb vertically from bottom to top
with the 1-1/2" comb. Move the comb 1/4" to
one side and comb back down from top to bottom, forming another cable over the whole pattern. The vertical cable will be dominant.

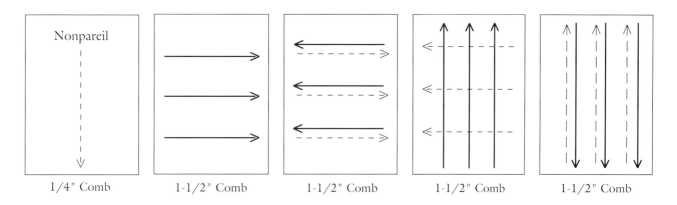

CHEVRON

The difference between chevron and getgel is mainly the size of the pattern. However, when you make two full getgels with a 3" (7.5 cm) rake and then comb back and forth again with a 1" (2.5 cm) comb, the getgel becomes not only smaller but also more delicate. Chevron is a useful pattern, able to suggest both flames and plant and flower forms.

As with the nonpareil, compound patterns can be created on a chevron base. Chevron has no up-and-down directional flow—it's the same pattern both ways. If you make a bouquet over a chevron, for example, the final pattern is the same as if you had made a reverse bouquet over a chevron.

Because it takes considerable time to complete a chevron pattern, dust can become a problem. Holes in the pattern made by dust particles show up most on a finely combed pattern such as a feathered chevron. Doing chevron variations on a rainy day will help to minimize dust contamination.

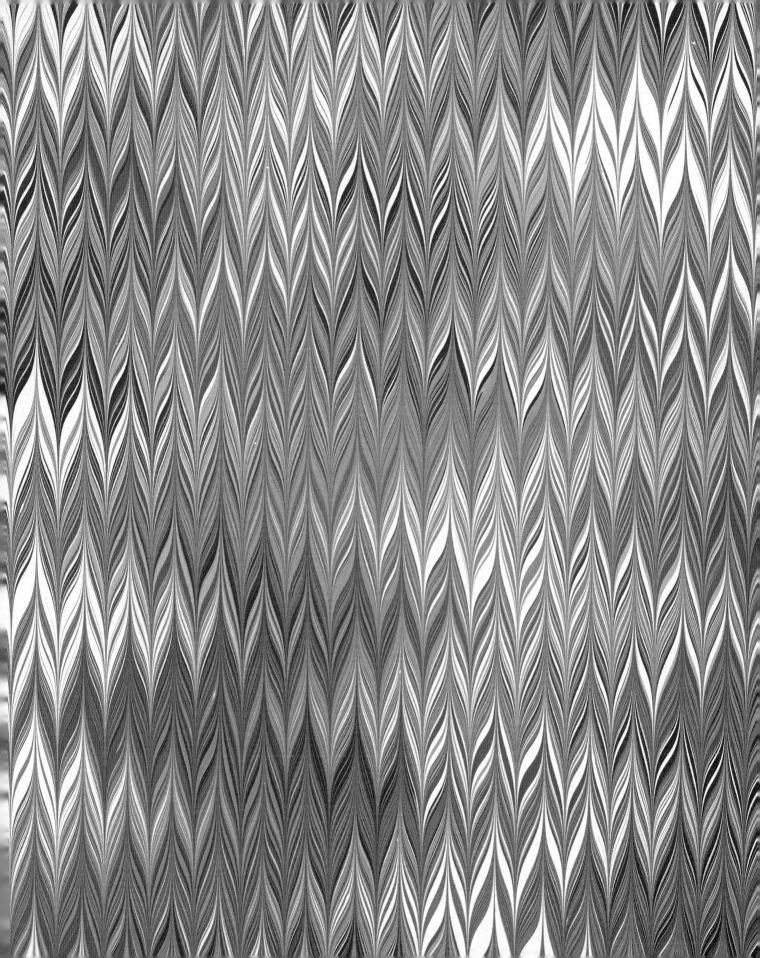

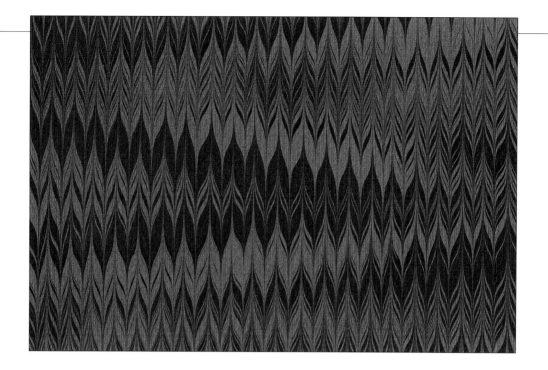

■ CHEVRON ■

Start with a horizontal getgel. Then comb vertically from bottom to top, using either a 1/2" (1 cm) comb, as in the large sample, or a 1/4" (6 mm) comb, as in the small sample above. Then use the same comb to comb from top to bottom, bisecting the lines of the last stroke. These movements should be made slowly. Fast movements create a ripple in the bath, making it hard to keep the lines in registration. *Note:* Keep your eye on only one tooth of the comb as you make the last stroke; it is easier to see whether you are staying evenly between the lines of the previous stroke.

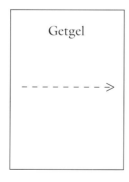

Getgel

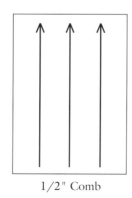

1/2" Comb

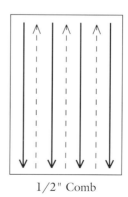

1/2" Comb

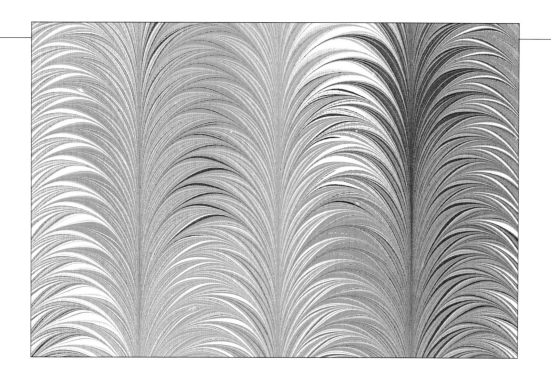

▪ PALM ▪

Also called a fern pattern, this design actually resembles the top of a pineapple. For the large sample at left, begin with a horizontal chevron made with a 1/2" (1 cm) comb. Rake the chevron top to bottom with a 2" (5 cm) rake. To make the small sample above, use a 1/4" (6 mm) chevron and a 1-1/2" (4 cm) comb for the vertical raking movement.

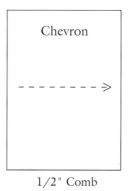

1/2" Comb

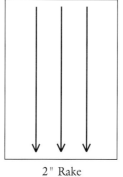

2" Rake

▪ FLAME ▪

Start with a horizontal chevron made with a 1"
(2.5 cm) rake. Then, for the large sample at left,
rake vertically from top to bottom with a 3" (7.5
cm) rake, moving in a gentle wave. For the small
sample above, make the chevron with a 1/2"
(1 cm) comb, then use a 2" (5 cm) rake.

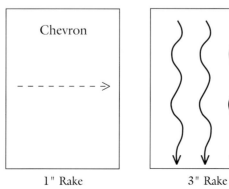

Chevron

1" Rake   3" Rake

▪ F E A T H E R E D   C H E V R O N ▪

First make a vertical chevron, using a 1" (2.5 cm) rake. Then make a horizontal waved getgel over it—that is, rake left to right with a 3" (7.5 cm) rake, then rake right to left with the same tool, bisecting the lines of the first stroke and using a gentle waved motion for the last pass of the rake.

To make the small sample above, use a 1/2" chevron and a 2" (5 cm) rake.

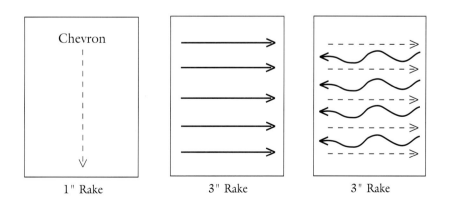

■ COCKATOO ■

First make a vertical chevron, using a 1/2" (1 cm) comb. Then rake horizontally from left to right with a 2" (5 cm) rake. Finally, rake from top to bottom with the 2" rake. To make the smaller sample above, again start with a 1/2" chevron, but use a 1-1/2" (4 cm) comb for additional movements.

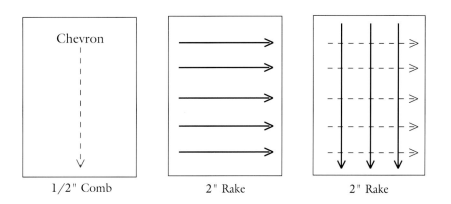

Chevron

1/2" Comb   2" Rake   2" Rake

▪ FLEUR DE LIS ▪

Also called a lily, artichoke, and bouquet chevron, this pattern begins with a vertical chevron made with a 1/2" (1 cm) comb. Use the bouquet comb vertically over the chevron, moving from top to bottom in an elongated S motion. To make the small sample above, start with a 1/4" (6 mm) chevron and use a smaller bouquet comb.

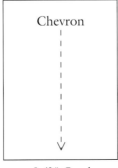

Chevron

1/2" Comb

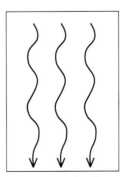

Bouquet Comb

■ OCTOPUS ■

Begin with a vertical chevron made with a 1/2"
(1 cm) comb. Rake horizontally from left to right
with a 3" (7.5 cm) rake, moving in a rhythmic wave.
Then rake back across the bath from right to left,
using the same motion and crossing the first lines to
produce a series of horizontal figure eights. For the
small sample above, use a 1-1/2" (4 cm) comb to
make the horizontal figure eights. Basically, this pattern is an angel's wing movement over a chevron.

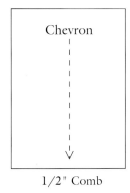

1/2" Comb

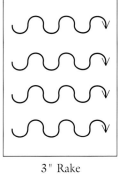

3" Rake

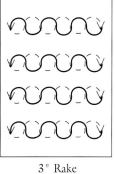

3" Rake

▪ CURLED CHEVRON ▪

Start with a vertical chevron made with a 1/2"
(1 cm) comb. Use the bouquet comb to make the
curls, moving from the outer edge to the center of
each curl. Alternatively, make the curls with a 2" (5
cm) rake, one row at a time, making sure to stagger
the rows. Isolated curls can be made with a stylus,
as in the small sample above.

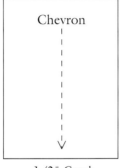

Chevron

1/2" Comb

Bouquet Comb

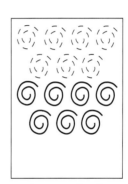

Bouquet Comb

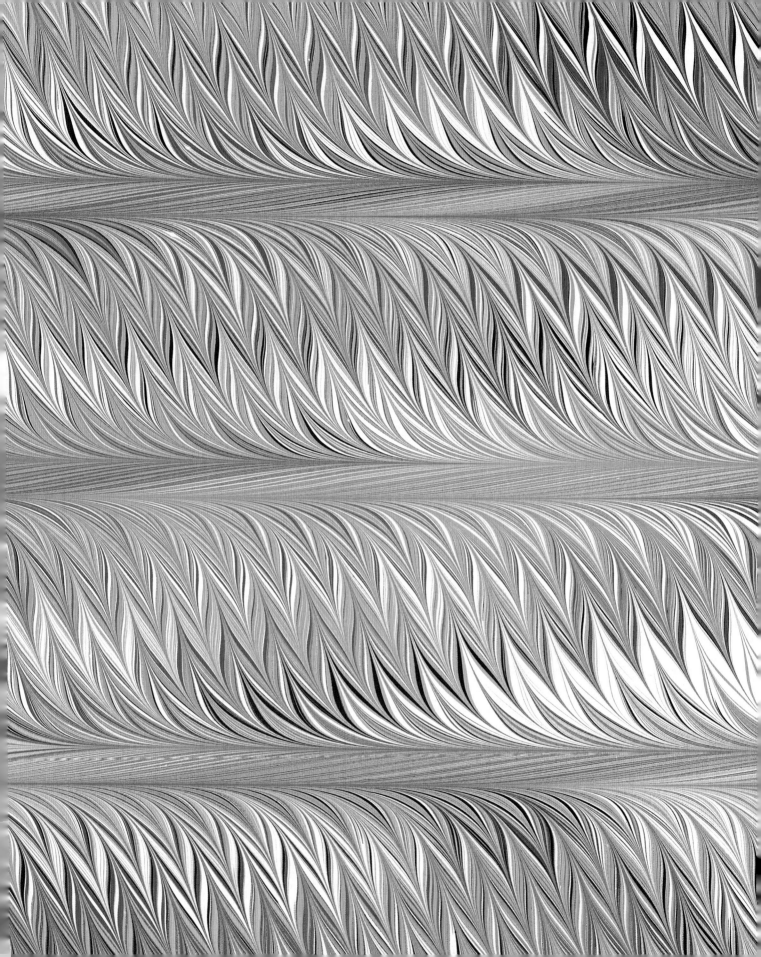

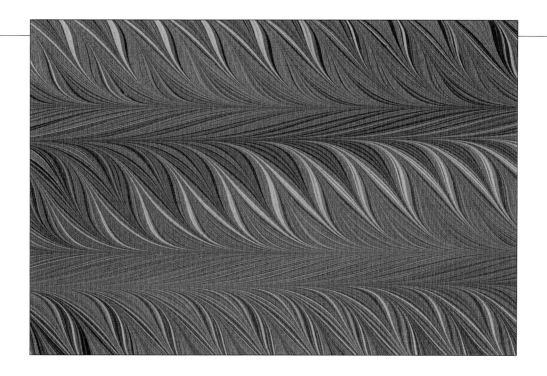

▪ CABLED CHEVRON ▪

Using a 1" (2.5 cm) rake, make a vertical chevron.
Use a 3" (7.5 cm) rake to make horizontal cables
over the chevron, shifting the rake up 1/4" (6 mm)
for the return stroke. To make the small sample
above, again use a 1/2" chevron, but then use a
1-1/2" comb for the cable.

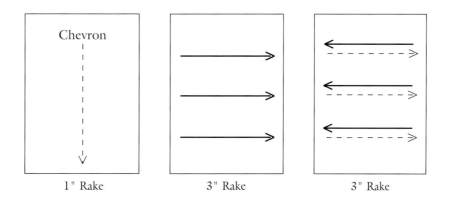

1" Rake   3" Rake   3" Rake

▪ DOUBLE CABLED CHEVRON ▪

For the large sample at left, begin with a vertical chevron made with a 1/2" (1 cm) comb. Make horizontal cables with a 1-1/2" (4 cm) comb, spacing 1/4" (6 mm) between movements. Cable vertically with the same comb, again spacing 1/4" away for the return movement.

For the small sample above, make a vertical chevron with a 1" (2.5 cm) rake and make the cables with a 1-1/2" (4 cm) comb.

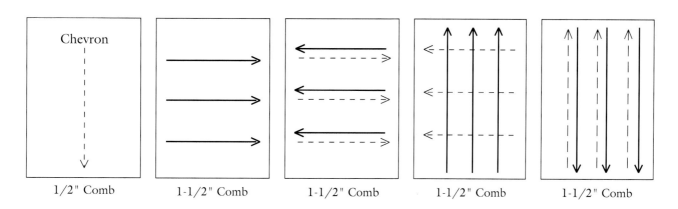

Chevron				
1/2" Comb	1-1/2" Comb	1-1/2" Comb	1-1/2" Comb	1-1/2" Comb

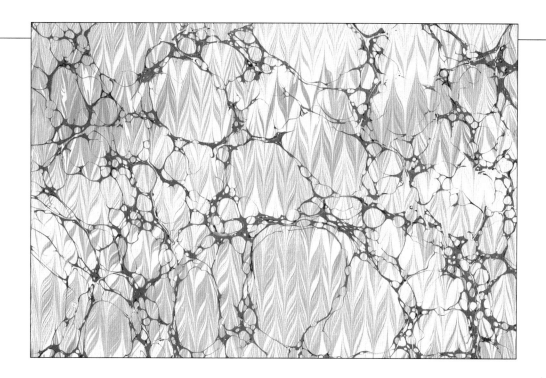

■ OVERMARBLE ■

This technique is also known as ghost marble
and phantom marble. The paper is marbled once
and allowed to dry. Then it is re-alumed and marbled again. Even more images can be marbled on
top of the second one. The technique has endless
possibilities, and is also an excellent way to save an
undesirable piece of marbling: just marble it again.
  To make the pattern shown in the large sample
at left, make a horizontal getgel, using a 2" (5 cm)
rake. For the second marble, make a vertical getgel,
also with a 2" rake. For the small sample above,
make a 1/4" (6 mm) vertical chevron and over-
marble it with an Italian hair vein pattern.

MANY MARBLERS' MARBLING
MARBLING AS FINE ART

As has so often happened in the history of this ancient art, once again there is a resurgence of interest in marbling. In contrast to past experiences, this late-20th-century renaissance is marked by openness and sharing of information, instead of secrecy. There are many qualified marblers teaching marbling and there are "gatherings" of marblers sharing their knowledge and demonstrating their techniques. In just the past decade there have been more than a dozen major exhibitions devoted to marbling, most with international participation.

Because of our instant communication and the ease of modern travel, this is an international renaissance, marching across borders and moving aside language barriers into a new era of marbling. This chapter showcases some of the exciting, contemporary work now being done. It also illustrates how marbling has moved from its traditional use in books into art galleries and museums, where it stands on its own in a very distinctive way.

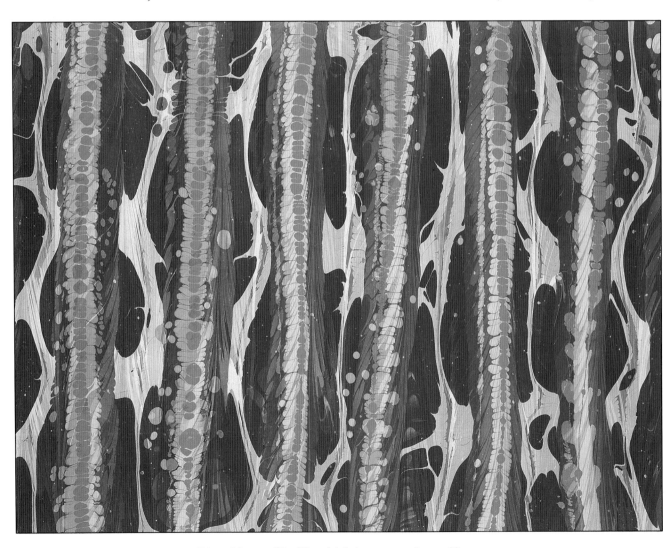

*Diane Maurer, "Reef," multiple-image gouache marbling
on carragheenan, 1991, 23" x 27" (57.5 x 67.5 cm).*

Kay Radcliffe, "The Oriental,"
drawing over oil marbling,
8" x 8-1/2" (20 x 21 cm).

Wendy Medeiros, Untitled,
oil paints on carragheenan,
1989, 20" x 24" (50 x 60 cm).

Right: Milena Hughes, "Vessel II," acrylics on paper, hand-painted over undulating fissure pattern, 1989, 19" x 25" (47.5 x 62.5 cm).

Below: Susan Pogány, "Visitors," watercolors on carragheenan, 1990, 18" x 24" (45 x 60 cm).

*Right: Michael Hughey and Mimi Schleicher, "Opulence."
Calligraphy: ink, gouache, and gold. Marbling: watercolors
on carragheenan. 1989. 21-1/2" x 23-3/4" (54 x 59 cm).*

*Below left: Christopher Weimann, "Indian Weave,"
acrylics, 1978, 19" x 24-3/4" (47.5 x 62 cm).*

*Below right: Mimi Schleicher, "Thorns," watercolors
on carragheenan, 1992, 8" x 21" (20 x 52.5 cm).*

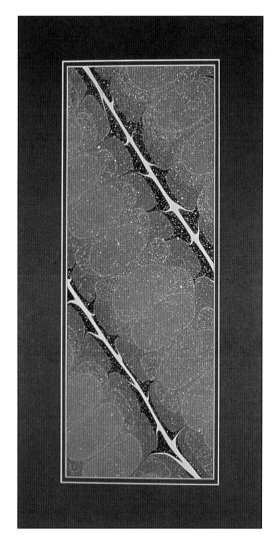

Tom Leech, "Midnight Rhyme,"
acrylic paints over metallic
underpaint, 1991,
20" x 24" (50 x 60 cm).

Eileen Canning, "Hieroglyph Arabesque,"
watercolors on carragheenan, 1983,
24" x 26" (60 x 65 cm).

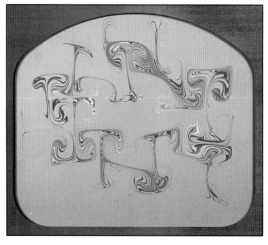

Karli Frigge, "Marbled Flowers," overmarbled with watercolors on carragheenan, 1970, 20" x 28" (50 x 70 cm). Joppe, Netherlands.

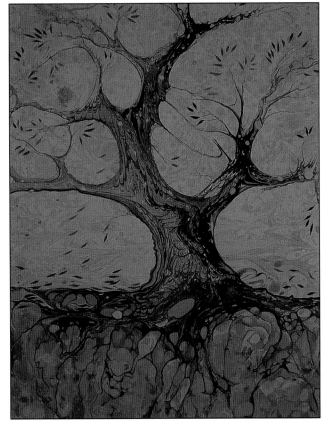

Dedree Drees, "Tree: Fall," watercolors on carragheenan, 1988, 18" x 23" (45 x 57.5 cm).

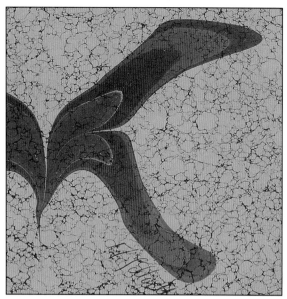

Mimi Schleicher, "Papillons," watercolors on carragheenan, overmarbled, 1991, 13" x 20" (32.5 x 50 cm). (Left: Detail).

Polly Fox, "Maybe, Tomorrow…,"
watercolors on carragheenan,
1993, 6″ x 9″ (15 x 22.5 cm).

Geert van Daal, Marbled Flower,
watercolors on carragheenan, 1989.
Dodewaard, Netherlands.

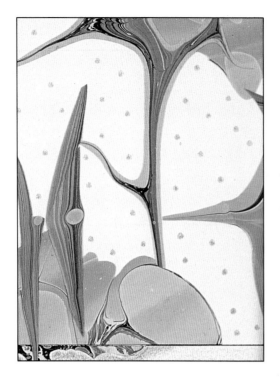

Patty Schleicher, "Extraterrestrial Landscape,"
1992, collage of watercolor marbling,
4-1/2" x 6-1/4" (11.25 x 15.5 cm).

Eva Clifford Kocq van Breugel,
"Tiger Eye Flowers," watercolors on
carragheenan, 1992, 17" x 23-1/2"
(42 x 59 cm). Driebergen, Netherlands.

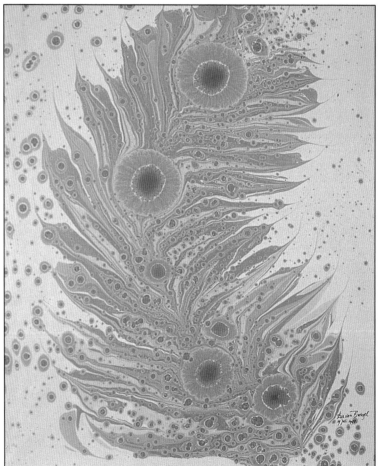

Iris Nevins, "Marbled Flowers,"
watercolors on carragheenan,
1992, 11" x 14" (27.5 x 35 cm).

Patty Schleicher, "Sun, Moon, and Stars,"
double collage cover of coptic-sewn address book,
1991, 6-1/4 x 8-1/4 (15-1/2 x 20-1/2 cm).

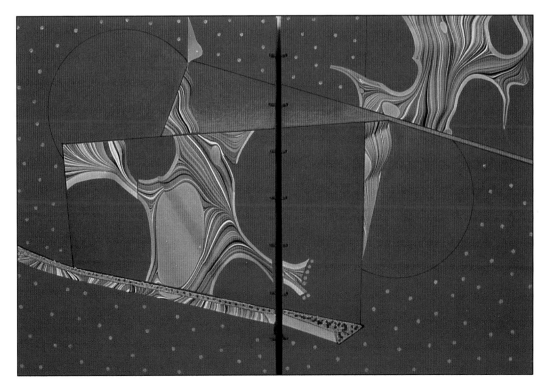

Laura Sims, "Sea Sections," watercolors on carragheenan size using comb contaminated with acrylic paints, 1990, 17" x 21" (42.5 x 52.5 cm).

Lia van Daal, Untitled, watercolors on carragheenan. Dodewaard, Netherlands.

SUPPLY SOURCES

MARBLING SUPPLIES

Boku-Undo USA, Inc.
594 Broadway, Ste 1003
New York, NY 10012
(212) 226-0988

Colophon Book Arts Supply
3046 Hogum Bay Road SE
Olympia, WA 98506
(206) 459-2940

Decorative Papers
Box 749
East Hampton, MA 01027
(413) 527-6103

Diane Maurer
P.O. Box 78
Spring Mills, PA 16875

Earth Guild
33 Haywood St.
Asheville, NC 28801
(800) 327-8448

TALAS
213 West 35th St.
New York, NY 10001
(212) 736-7744

MARBLED PAPER AND PAPER PRODUCTS

Crescent Cardboard
100 W. Willow Rd., Box X
Wheeling, IL 60090

Inklings…Creative Marbling
34 Wall St.
Asheville, NC 28801
(704) 252-3155

Schleicher Hand-Marbled Paper
Box 1005
Weaverville, NC 28787
(704) 645-5392

TALAS
213 West 35th St.
New York, NY 10001
(212) 736-774

MARBLING JOURNAL

Ink and Gall
Box 1469
Taos, NM 87571
(505) 586-1607

BOOKS ON MARBLING

Marblers' Bookshelf
Box 146
Taos, NM 87571

PAPER

Amsterdam Art
1013 University Ave.
Berkeley, CA 94710
(415) 548-9663

Daniel Smith, Inc.
4130 First Ave. S.
Seattle, WA 98134
(800) 426-6740

Stephen Kinsella, Inc.
P.O. Box 32420
Olivette, MO 63132
(800) 445-8865

SILK

Qualin International
P.O. Box 31145
San Francisco, CA 94131
(415) 647-1329

Thai Silks
252 State St.
Los Altos, Ca 94022
(800) 722-SILK

CALLIGRAPHY PRODUCTS

Twin Dolphin Press
P.O. Box 18122
Asheville, NC 28814
(704) 252-8800
Catalog $2.00

As a courtesy,
please send SASE
with inquiry.

BIBLIOGRAPHY

Campana, Michele. *Oriental Carpets*. London: Hamlyn, 1969.

Easton, Phoebe Jane. *Marbling: A History and a Bibliography*. Los Angeles, CA: Dawson's Bookshop, 1983.

Gauthier, Marie Madeleine. *Highways of the Faith*. Switzerland: J.A. Underwood, 1983.

Halfer, Joseph. *The Progress of the Marbling Art*. Facsimile of 1893 edition. Taos, NM: Columbine Printing, Inc., 1989.

Jackle-Sonmez, Yvonne. *Ebru: Turkish Marbled Paper*. Tubingen, Germany: 1987.

Loring, Rosamund B. *Decorated Book Papers*. Cambridge, MA: Harvard College Library, 1973.

Maurer, Diane. *Marbling*. New York: Crescent Books, 1991.

Miura, Einen. *The Art of Marbled Paper*. English edition. London: Zaehnsdorf, LTD., 1989.

Nevins, Iris. *Traditional Marbling*. Privately published, 1985

———. *Varieties of Spanish Marbling*. Bird and Bull Press, 1991.

Rice, David Talbot. *Art of the Byzantine Era*. London: Thames and Hudson, 1963.

Schleicher, Patty. *Marbling with Oil Colors*. Self-published, 1984. Available from the author, P.O. Box 1005, Weaverville, NC 28787.

Schwenk, Theodor. *Sensitive Chaos*. New York: Schocken Books, 1976.

Taylor, Carol, with Patty Schleicher, Mimi Schleicher, and Laura Sims. *Marbling Paper and Fabric*. New York: Sterling Publishing, 1991.

Titley, Norah M. *Persian Miniature Painting*. University of Texas Press, 1984.

Weimann, Ingrid, and Nedim Sönmez. *Christopher Weimann: A Tribute*. Türbigen, Germany: Jäckle-Sönmez, 1991.

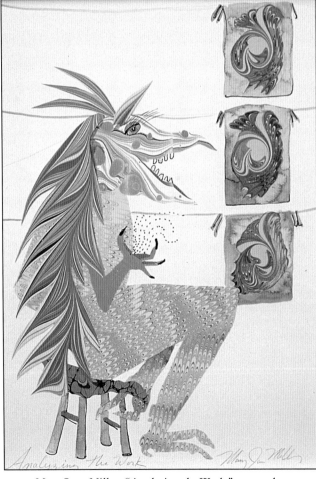

Mary Jane Miller, "Analyzing the Work," watercolors on carragheenan, collage, 1992, 9-1/2" x 13" (24 x 32 cm).

SUBJECT INDEX

INDEX OF PATTERNS